Louise Perry is a writer,
New Statesman columnist
and campaigner against
male sexual violence.

'Those feminists who assume this book is not for them – give it a go. Brilliantly written, cleverly argued, packed with fascinating ideas and information: agree or disagree with the central premise, it is fresh and exciting.'

Julie Bindel, feminist and writer,
author of *Feminism for Women*

'This is a marvellously essential book, brilliantly argued. Perry has written the most radical feminist challenge to a failed liberal feminism. For love of womankind, and based on her profound reading of scientific, cultural and historical material, Perry has committed heresy; namely, she has dared argue that men and women really are different, especially sexually – and that the so-called sexual revolution failed women, especially young and poor women, and in a most spectacular way. Hook-up culture, or "having sex like a man", is hardly liberating for most girls and women. What Perry has to say about pornography, prostitution and the uber eroticization of culture is both true and heartbreaking – but she is, perhaps, at her best, her kindest, when she writes about feminism and motherhood, about what both children and older women need in order to survive and flourish. Brava for such good writing and for such bold common sense.'

Phyllis Chesler, writer, feminist and psychologist,
author of *Women and Madness*

'Brilliantly conceived and written, this highly original book is an urgent call for a sexual counter-revolution. A book as stimulating as the splash of icy water that wakes someone from a nightmare.'

Helen Joyce, author of *Trans: When Ideology Meets Reality*

'Perry tackles the costs of the sexual revolution head-on. Wending her careful way through liberal narratives of progress and conservative hand-wringing over decline, Perry demonstrates that beginning with the priorities of women changes too how we must think about politics. Perry is a clear-sighted and unflinching guide through all of the major areas of contemporary sexual politics, from dating to marriage and children, pornography, and violence against women. We live, she suggests, in an era of "sexual disenchantment". What we need today is a new morality, a new set of virtues: the sexual revolution failed, but women and children were the greater losers. This is a brave and unflinching book: we have it in us to treat each other once more with dignity, Perry suggests. The party's over – long live love, virtue, commitment and kindness.'

Nina Power, author of *What Do Men Want?*

'For a generation now, we have been sold the lie that feminism means celebrating "sex work", violent pornography and casual hook-ups. To feel otherwise brands a woman not just as uncool and uptight but as an enemy of social justice. How the hell did the misogynist global sex trade manage to enlist feminism as head cheerleader? Enter the laser intellect of Louise Perry, who, in this thoughtful, timely and witty book, exposes the travesty of "sex positive" feminism as neither positive nor sexy and argues for new thinking that puts women's true interests, desires and happiness at its heart.'

Janice Turner, *Times* columnist and feature writer

The Case Against the
Sexual Revolution

For the women who learned it the hard way

The Case Against the Sexual Revolution

A New Guide to Sex in the 21st Century

LOUISE PERRY

polity

First published in 2022 by Polity Press

Polity Press
65 Bridge Street
Cambridge CB2 1UR, UK

Polity Press
101 Station Landing
Suite 300
Medford, MA 02155, USA

ISBN-13: 978-1-5095-4998-6
ISBN-13: 978-1-5095-4999-3 (pb)

A catalogue record for this book is available from the British Library.

Library of Congress Control Number: 2021953231

Typeset in 11 on 13 pt Sabon
by Cheshire Typesetting Ltd, Cuddington, Cheshire
Printed and bound in Great Britain by TJ Books Ltd, Padstow, Cornwall

The publisher has used its best endeavours to ensure that the URLs for external websites referred to in this book are correct and active at the time of going to press. However, the publisher has no responsibility for the websites and can make no guarantee that a site will remain live or that the content is or will remain appropriate.

Every effort has been made to trace all copyright holders, but if any have been overlooked the publisher will be pleased to include any necessary credits in any subsequent reprint or edition.

For further information on Polity, visit our website:
politybooks.com

Contents

Acknowledgements   vi
Foreword by Kathleen Stock   viii

1. Sex Must Be Taken Seriously   1
2. Men and Women Are Different   21
3. Some Desires Are Bad   45
4. Loveless Sex Is Not Empowering   70
5. Consent Is Not Enough   94
6. Violence Is Not Love   114
7. People Are Not Products   135
8. Marriage Is Good   161
   Conclusion: Listen to Your Mother   186

Notes   191

Acknowledgements

I owe enormous thanks to my agent, Matthew Hamilton, and my editor, George Owers, without whom this book would never have been written. I am also indebted to the many people who read and commented on various proposals and drafts: Julie Bindel, Diana Fleischman, David Goodhart, Camille Guillot, Jessica Masterson, Dina McMillan, Nina Power, Katharina Rietzler, Rajiv Shah, Kathleen Stock and Randy Thornhill. I owe particular thanks to the brilliant Mary Harrington, who provided constant support and ideas, and to my other 'reactionary' feminist friends: Alex Kaschuta, Katherine Dee, Helen Roy and Mason Hartman. I am eternally grateful to Fiona MacKenzie, my friend and colleague, who founded We Can't Consent to This. And I owe thanks also to Eve and Max for sticking by me, despite my terrible opinions – I really do appreciate it.

I depend, as ever, on the love and companionship of my husband and family, including my beloved son, who was born during the writing of this book, and my most faithful reader, my mum, who has read every word I've ever published.

The little respect paid to chastity in the male world is, I am persuaded, the grand source of many of the physical and moral evils that torment mankind, as well as of the vices and follies that degrade and destroy women.

Mary Wollstonecraft, *A Vindication of the Rights of Woman*

he said they'd found a brothel
on the dig he did last night

I asked him how they know

he sighed:

a pit of babies' bones
a pit of newborn babies' bones was how to spot a brothel

Hollie McNish, 'Conversation with an archeologist'

Foreword
by Kathleen Stock

What did the sexual revolution of the 1960s ever do for us? In this brilliant book, Louise Perry argues that it depends which 'us' you're talking about. The invention of the contraceptive pill reduced women's fear of unwanted pregnancy, enabling them to provide the kind of sex a lot of men prefer: copious and commitment-free. Many women claim to enjoy this kind of sex too. But, as Perry explains, there's good reason to disbelieve at least some such reports. For we now live in a culture where, though it isn't taboo for a man to choke a woman during sex, or anally penetrate her, or ejaculate on her face while filming it, it *is* taboo for a young woman to express discomfort about the nature of the sexual bargain she's expected by society to make. This bargain says: sacrifice your own wellbeing for the pleasures of men in order to compete in the heterosexual dating marketplace at all.

As Perry documents in sometimes shocking vignettes, whatever ill effects the sexual revolution had for women in the twentieth century have been supersized in the digital age of the twenty-first. There is little doubt that contemporary sexual culture is destructive for younger women in particular. It sells them a sexbot aesthetic, pressures them into promiscuity, bombards them with dick pics and violent pornography, and tells them to enjoy being humiliated and assaulted in bed. It says that, as long as they choose it, being exploited for money is 'sex work' and that 'sex work is work'. It also tells women not to mix up sex with love and to stay disconnected and emotionless from partners. It encourages them to change their bodies in ways that match pornographic ideals. And, worst of all, it says that to comply with all of this is empowering – ignoring the obvious fact that telling women to subdue their minds and submit their bodies to physically stronger strangers can be lethal.

Perhaps surprisingly, the taboo around discussing the costs of the sexual revolution is enabled by popular feminism. This is because popular feminism is a version of liberal feminism, and liberal feminism in its populist guise is focused mostly on a woman's 'right to choose' or 'consent', construed incredibly thinly. Everything and anything goes as long as you choose or consent to it at the time. What this misses out, of course, is that people can be pressured – by peers or partners or wider cultural forces – into believing that they want things which later they come to recognise as bad for them. In a culture dominated by male sexuality, there's an obvious interest in convincing women that they want to have sex like men do, and many women go along with things they later come to regret.

At this point, the inner liberal feminist in many readers may be howling: but what if I genuinely *want* all that stuff? Well, good for you if you genuinely do. But, as Perry shows, even if this sort of sex works for some women, there are many other women for whom it does not. And they aren't 'prudes', or 'frigid', or 'asexual', or 'in a moral panic', or any of the other insulting words produced by the culture to keep the whole man-pleasing machinery working. Nor need they be religious. There are plenty of reasons to be wary of contemporary sexual mores that are perfectly secular.

Both liberal feminism's narrow focus on choice and its incapacity to discuss deep differences between women and men stem from its intellectual forefather: liberalism, a political tradition heavily focused on freedom of choice as the thing definitive of personhood. The fantasy of a liberal subject is of an ostensibly sexless individual, defined mostly by the presence of a free will, untethered by family ties or community expectations and pursuing private preferences in a relatively unfettered way. I say 'ostensibly sexless', because – in a point made by second-wave feminists and brought up to date by Perry – this idealised figure of a liberal subject sounds more like a man roaming around getting his oats than a woman whose life is intertwined with the kids that are the outcome of her own sexual activity.

How then can we start talking about what might work for women, specifically? Perry turns to biology and evolutionary psychology, asking: What does a woman tend to desire, given the kind of female animal she is, with the specific reproductive capacities she tends to have? (Talk of animals is not insulting. We are all animals, though hubris tries to make us forget it.) Given the vexed history of discussion about nature vs nurture within feminism, this move towards the natural is a bold one. But Perry's approach deserves open-minded attention – especially when you remember that, according to the currently more popular narrative, human bodies as well as minds are plastic. Yes: such is liberal feminism's fear of limits upon personal freedom that – in tandem with its BFF capitalism – it now construes facts about healthy bodies as obstacles to freedom. Don't like your breasts? Buy new ones, or cut them off altogether! (Delete as appropriate.) Incredibly, in some feminists, the degree of denial stretches even to telling us that biology itself is a myth or a construct. Yet, as Perry argues, once we acknowledge the 'hard limits imposed by biology', we can make informed inferences about female wellbeing in particular – rooted in the real, and not what is projected or fantasised by men.

Perry's background as a journalist, commentator, and campaigner against 'rough sex' criminal defences perfectly places her to tackle these issues, and she does so with characteristic style and fearlessness. Her book does several things that are unusual for a modern feminist text. It refuses the easy wins of the Cool Girl Feminist, swimming against the pink tide of sex-positive vacuity to spell out some uncomfortable truths. It is uninterested in liberal feminist buzzwords such as freedom and equality, focusing instead on women's needs and wellbeing, independently from a consideration of men. Whether you ultimately agree or disagree with Perry's analysis, the book takes the interests of women deadly seriously and carves out a space for them to talk properly about the costs of the sexual culture in which they must sink or swim. It's essential for the wellbeing of young women that we do this, and we should all be grateful to Perry for advancing this important conversation.

1

Sex Must Be Taken Seriously

Hugh Hefner and Marilyn Monroe – those two icons of the sexual revolution – never actually met, but they were born in the same year and laid to rest in the same place, side by side.[1] In 1992, Hefner bought the crypt next door to Monroe's in the Westwood Memorial Park Cemetery in Los Angeles for $75,000,[2] telling the *Los Angeles Times*: 'I'm a believer in things symbolic . . . [so] spending eternity next to Marilyn is too sweet to pass up.'[3] At the age of ninety-one, Hefner got his wish. The long-dead Monroe had no say in the matter. But then she had never been given much say in what men did to her over the course of her short life.

Marilyn Monroe was both the first ever cover star and the first ever naked centrefold in the first ever edition of Hefner's *Playboy* magazine, published in December 1953. 'Entertainment for MEN' was the promise offered on the front cover, and the magazine evidently delivered on that promise, since it was a commercial success from its very first issue.

Marilyn Monroe's naked photos were four years old by the time of their publication. In 1949, the 23-year-old Monroe had been paid $50 for a two-hour photo shoot with pin-up photographer Tom Kelley, who had promised that he'd make her unrecognisable, and almost delivered on his promise.[4] The woman curled up on a red velvet bedspread is not obviously Monroe, since her hair was a little more brunette at the time, her pained face was half hidden behind an outstretched arm, and her pale, pretty body was indistinguishable from the bodies of most of the other models in *Playboy* (which would not feature a black centrefold until 1965 – the eighteen-year-old recipient of this dubious honour, Jennifer Jackson, later described 'Hef' as 'a high-class pimp').[5]

The clothed Monroe on the cover of the magazine beckoned in readers with the promise of a 'FULL COLOR' nude photo of the actress for the 'first time in any magazine', and Hefner later said that her centrefold was the key reason for the publication's initial success. Monroe herself was humiliated by the photo shoot, which she resorted to only out of desperate need for money, signing the release documents with a fake name.[6] Hefner didn't pay her to use her images and didn't seek her consent before publishing them.[7] Monroe reportedly told a friend that she had 'never even received a thank-you from all those who made millions off a nude Marilyn photograph. I even had to buy a copy of the magazine to see myself in it.'[8]

The courses of these two lives show us in perfect vignette the nature of the sexual revolution's impact on men and women. Monroe and Hefner both began in obscurity and ended their lives rich and famous, having found success in the same city and at the very same historical moment. But, while Hefner lived a long, grubby life in his mansion with his playmates, Monroe's life was cut short by misery and substance abuse. As the radical feminist Andrea Dworkin later wrote:

> She grinned, she posed, she pretended, she had affairs with famous and powerful men. A friend of hers claimed that she had so many illegal abortions wrongly performed that her reproductive organs were severely injured. She died alone, possibly acting on her own behalf for the first time . . . Her lovers in

both flesh and fantasy had fucked her to death, and her apparent suicide stood at once as accusation and answer: no, Marilyn Monroe, the ideal sexual female, had not liked it.[9]

Monroe's life followed a similar trajectory to that of her pin-up predecessor Bettie Page, who survived into old age but spent her final decades in a psychiatric institution. So too the pop star Britney Spears, who at the age of sixteen gyrated in a school uniform and begged viewers to 'hit me baby one more time'. Spears has since suffered a protracted and very public nervous breakdown, just like the countless other Monroes – some of whom we will meet over the course of this book – who have been destroyed in much the same way as the original icon.

In particular, today's female porn performers – the most successful of whom now inhabit much the same cultural space that Monroe inhabited in her day – are far more likely than their peers to have been sexually abused as children, to have been in foster care, and to have been victims of domestic violence as adults[10] – all misfortunes that Monroe suffered too.[11] The libidinous public asks a lot of the women it desires. And when it all goes horribly wrong, as it usually does, this public labels these once-desired women 'crazy' and moves on. There is never a reckoning with what sexual liberation does to those women who follow its directives most obediently.

Hugh Hefner experienced 'sexual liberation' very differently from Monroe, as men typically do, although his example is no more worthy of emulation. As a younger man, he was the true playboy – handsome, charming and envied by other men. He lived the fantasy of a particularly immature adolescent boy, hosting parties for his celebrity friends in a garish 'grotto' and then retiring upstairs with his harem of identical twenty-something blondes. He supposedly once said that his best pick-up line was simply the sentence 'Hi, my name is Hugh Hefner.'[12]

Unlike Monroe, Hefner lived to grow old and, as he did so, lost much of his glitter. By the end of his life, he was more often publicly portrayed as a pathetic figure, and various former playmates provided the press with unflattering accounts of life in the Playboy mansion. Jill Ann Spaulding, for instance, wrote of the elderly Hefner's uninspiring sexual performance: 'Hef just lies there with his Viagra erection. It's just a fake erection, and each girl gets on top of him for two minutes while the girls in the background try to keep him excited. They'll yell things like, "Fuck her daddy, fuck her daddy!"'[13]

Other women spoke of soiled mattresses, a bizarre playmate uniform of matching pink flannel pyjamas, and carpets covered with dog faeces.[14] It was revealed that Hefner took an obsessive and coercive attitude towards his many girlfriends, dictating how they wore their hair and make-up, keeping a detailed log of all his sexual encounters,[15] and becoming angry if refused sex.[16] His acolytes forgave 'Hef' when he was still young and attractive, but as time went on he was revealed to be little more than a dirty old man. The glamour of the playboy – or the 'fuckboy', in modern slang – doesn't last forever.

Hefner's reputation may have diminished over time, but he never experienced any guilt for the harm he perpetrated. Asked at the age of eighty-three by the *New York Times* if he regretted any of the 'dark consequences' of the *Playboy* revolution he set in motion, Hefner was confident in his innocence: 'it's a small price to pay for personal freedom.'[17] By which he meant, of course, personal freedom for men like him.

After his death in 2017, the original playboy was described again and again in the press as a 'complex figure'. The *Huffington Post* wrote of his 'contradictory feminist legacy',[18] and the BBC asked 'was the Playboy revolution good for women?'[19] One British journalist argued that Hefner had 'helped push feminism forwards':

[Hefner] took a particularly progressive stance to the contraceptive pill and abortion rights, which the magazine often plugged, and kept readers up-to-date with the struggles women were facing; leading up to the legalisation of abortion in 1973, Playboy featured at least 30 different commentaries on the Roe V. Wade case and large features from doctors.[20]

None of these eulogists seemed to recognise that Hefner's commitment to decoupling reproduction from sex had nothing to do with a commitment to women's wellbeing. Hefner never once campaigned for anything that didn't bring him direct benefit, and, when fear of pregnancy was one of the last remaining reasons for women saying 'no', he had every reason to wish for a change that would widen the pool of women available to him.

Marilyn Monroe was scraped out again and again by backstreet abortionists because she died almost a decade before the Pill was made available to unmarried women in all American states. *Playboy* magazine existed for twenty years in a country without legalised abortion. The sexual revolution began in a society fresh from the horrors of the Second World War and enjoying a new form of affluence, but its outriders initially bore a lot of illegitimate children and suffered a lot of botched abortions. The 1966 film *Alfie* stars a gorgeous young Michael Caine bed-hopping around London and enjoying the libertine lifestyle promised by the swinging sixties. But his actions have consequences and, in the emotional climax of the film, Alfie cries as he is confronted with the grisly product of a backstreet abortion he has procured for one of his 'birds'.

The story of the sexual revolution isn't only a story of women freed from the burdens of chastity and motherhood, although it is that. It is also a story of the triumph of the playboy – a figure who is too often both forgotten and forgiven, despite his central role in this still recent history. Second-wave feminists were right to argue that women needed contraception and legalised abortion in order to give them control over their reproductive lives, and the arrival of this technology was a good and needful innovation, since it has freed so many women from the body-breaking work of unwanted childbearing. But the likes of Hefner also wanted this technology, and needed it, if they were to achieve the goal of liberating their own libidos while pretending that they were liberating women.

Sexual liberalism and its discontents

In Sophocles' *Antigone* – a play particularly attentive to the duty and suffering of women – the chorus sing that 'nothing that is vast enters into the life of mortals without a curse.' The societal impact of the Pill was vast and, two generations on, we haven't yet fully understood both its blessing and its curse. There have been plenty of periods in human history in which the norms around sex have been loosened: the late Roman Empire, Georgian Britain, and the Roaring Twenties in America are the best remembered. But these phases of licentiousness were self-limited by the lack of good contraception, and thus straight men in pursuit of extramarital sex were mostly obliged to seek out sex either with women in prostitution or with the small number of eccentric women who were willing to risk being cast out permanently from respectable society. The Bloomsbury set, for instance, who famously 'lived in squares and loved in triangles', had plenty of illicit sexual encounters. They also produced a lot of illegitimate children, and were protected from destitution only as a result of the privileges of their class.

But the sexual revolution of the 1960s stuck, and its ideology is now the ideological sea we swim in – so normalised that we can hardly see it for what it is. It was able to persist because of the arrival, for the first time in the history of the world, of reliable contraception and, in particular, forms of contraception that women could take charge of themselves, such as the Pill, the diaphragm, and subsequent improvements on the technology, such as the intrauterine device (IUD). Thus, at the end of the 1960s, an entirely new creature arrived in the world: the apparently fertile young woman whose fertility had in fact been put on hold. She changed everything.

This book is an attempt to reckon with that change, and to do so while avoiding the accounts typically offered by liberals addicted to a narrative of progress or conservatives addicted to a narrative of decline. I don't believe that the last sixty years or so should be understood as a period of exclusive progress or exclusive decline, because the sexual revolution has not freed *all* of us, but it has freed *some* of us, and selectively, and at a price. Which is exactly what we should expect from any form of social change 'that is vast', as this one certainly is. And although I am writing against a conservative narrative of the post-1960s era, and in particular those conservatives who are silly enough to think that returning to the 1950s is either possible or desirable, I am writing in a more deliberate and focused way against a liberal narrative of sexual liberation which I think is not only wrong but also harmful.

My complaint is focused more against liberals than against conservatives for a very personal reason: I used to believe the liberal narrative. As a younger woman, I held the same political opinions as most other millennial urban graduates in the West – in other words, I conformed to the beliefs of my class, including liberal feminist ideas about porn, BDSM, hook-up culture, evolutionary psychology, and the sex trade, which will all be addressed in this book. I let go of these beliefs because of my own life experiences, including a period immediately after university spent working at a rape crisis centre. If the old quip tells us that a 'conservative is just a liberal who has been mugged by reality', then I suppose, at least in my case, that a post-liberal feminist is just a liberal feminist who has witnessed the reality of male violence up close.

I'm using the term 'liberal feminism' to describe a form of feminism that is usually not described as such by its proponents, who nowadays are more likely to call themselves 'intersectional feminists'. But I don't think that their ideology actually *is* intersectional, according to Kimberlé Crenshaw's original meaning, in that it does not properly incorporate an analysis of other forms of social stratification, particularly economic class. The advantage of using 'liberal feminism' instead is that it places these twenty-first-century ideas within a longer intellectual history, making clear that this is a feminist iteration of a much grander intellectual project: liberalism.

The definition of 'liberalism' is contested – indeed, the first line of the Stanford Encyclopaedia of Philosophy entry tells us that 'liberalism is more than one thing' – which means that, whatever definition I choose to work with, I'll leave some critics unhappy. But I'm reluctant to bore readers by offering a long-winded defence of my working definition, so I'll be brief.

I'm not using 'liberal' as short-hand for 'left wing' – in fact, far from it. The American post-liberal political theorist Patrick Deneen describes economic liberalism and social liberalism as intertwined, with a liberal cultural elite and a liberal corporate elite working hand in hand: 'Today's corporate ideology has a strong affinity with the lifestyles of those who are defined by mobility, ethical flexibility, liberalism (whether economic or social), a consumerist mentality in which choice is paramount, and a "progressive" outlook in which rapid change and "creative destruction" are the only certainties.'[21]

Post-liberals such as Deneen draw attention to the costs of social liberalism, a political project that seeks to free individuals from the external constraints placed on us by location, family, religion, tradition, and even (and most relevant to feminists) the human body. In that sense, they are in agreement with many social conservatives. But post-liberals are also critical of the other side of the liberal coin: a free market ideology that seeks to free individuals from all of these constraints in order to maximise their ability to work and to consume. The atomised worker with no commitment to any place or person is the worker best able to respond quickly to the demands of the market. This ideal liberal subject can move to wherever the jobs are because she has no connection to anywhere in particular; she can do whatever labour is asked of her without any moral objection derived from faith or tradition; and, without a spouse or family to attend to, she never needs to demand rest days or a flexible schedule. And then, with the money earned from this rootless labour, she is able to buy consumables that will soothe any feelings of unhappiness, thus feeding the economic engine with maximum efficiency.

Liberal feminism takes this market-orientated ideology and applies it to issues specific to women. For instance, when the actress and campaigner Emma Watson was criticised in 2017 for showing her breasts on the cover of *Vanity Fair*, she hit back with a well-worn liberal feminist phrase: 'feminism is about giving women choice . . . It's about freedom.'[22] For liberal feminists such as Watson, that might mean the freedom to wear revealing clothes (and sell lots of magazines in the process), or the freedom to sell sex, or make or consume porn, or pursue whatever career you like, just like the boys.

With the right tools, freedom from the constraints imposed by the female body now becomes increasingly possible. Don't want to have children in your twenties or thirties? Freeze your eggs. Called away on a work trip postpartum? Fed-Ex your breastmilk to your newborn. Want to continue working full-time without interruption? Employ a live-in nanny, or – better yet – a surrogate who can bear the child for you. And now, with the availability of sex reassignment medical technologies, even stepping out of your female body altogether has become an option. Liberal feminism promises women freedom – and when that promise comes up against the hard limits imposed by biology, then the ideology directs women to chip away at those limits through the use of money, technology and the bodies of poorer people.

I don't reject the desire for freedom – I'm not an anti-liberal, and goodness knows that women have every reason to chafe against the constraints imposed on us by our societies and our bodies, both in the past and in the modern world. But I am critical of any ideology that fails to balance freedom against other values, and I'm also critical of the failure of liberal feminism to interrogate where our desire for a certain type of freedom comes from, too often referring back to a circular logic by which a woman's choices are good because she chooses them, just like *Sex and the City*'s Charlotte York yelping 'I choose my choice, I choose my choice!'

In this book I'm going to ask – and seek to answer – some questions about freedom that liberal feminism can't or won't answer: Why do so many women desire a kind of sexual freedom that so obviously serves male interests? What if our bodies and minds aren't as malleable as we might like to think? What do we lose when we prioritise freedom above all else? And, above all, *how should we act*, given all this?

Some of my conclusions might not be welcome, since they draw attention to the hard limits on our freedom that can't be surmounted, however much we try. And I start from a position that historically has often been a source of discomfort for feminists of all ideological persuasions: I accept the fact that men and women are different, and that those differences aren't going away. When we recognise these limits and these differences, then sexual politics takes on a different character. Instead of asking 'How can we all be free?', we must ask instead 'How can we best promote the wellbeing of both men and women, given that these two groups have different sets of interests, which are sometimes in tension?'

Sexual disenchantment

I'm going to argue in this book that Western sexual culture in the twenty-first century doesn't properly balance these interests – instead, it promotes the interests of the Hugh

Hefners of the world at the expense of the Marilyn Monroes. And the influence of liberal feminism means that too many women don't recognise this truth, blithely accepting Hefner's claim that all of the downsides of the new sexual culture are just 'a small price to pay for personal freedom'.

Which suits the likes of Hefner very nicely, since playboys like him have a lot to gain from the new sexual culture. It is in their interests to push a particularly radical idea about sex that has come out of the sexual revolution and has proved remarkably influential, despite its harms. This is the idea that sex is nothing more than a leisure activity, invested with meaning only if the participants choose to give it meaning. Proponents of this idea argue that sex has no intrinsic specialness, that it is not innately different from any other kind of social interaction, and that it can therefore be commodified without any trouble. The sociologist Max Weber described the 'disenchantment' of the natural world that resulted from the Enlightenment, as the ascendence of rationality stripped away the sense of magic that this 'enchanted garden' had once held for pre-modern people. In much the same way, sex has been disenchanted[23] in the post-1960s West, leaving us with a society that (ostensibly) believes that sex means nothing.

Sexual disenchantment is a natural consequence of the liberal privileging of freedom over all other values, because, if you want to be utterly free, you have to take aim at any kind of social restrictions that limit you, particularly the belief that sex has some unique, intangible value – some specialness that is difficult to rationalise. From this belief in the specialness of sex comes a host of potentially unwelcome phenomena, including patriarchal religious systems. But when we attempt to disenchant sex, and so pretend that this particular act is neither uniquely wonderful nor uniquely violating, then there is another kind of cost.

That cost falls disproportionately on women, for biological reasons that I'll come back to in the next chapter. And liberal feminists do seem to recognise this disproportionate impact, as demonstrated by the popularity of the Me Too movement, which began in earnest in 2017. This outpouring of rage and sorrow was evidence of a sexual culture that wasn't working for women. The stories that came out of Me Too included plenty of unambiguously criminal behaviour, but there were also a lot of women who described sexual encounters that were technically consensual but nevertheless left them feeling terrible because they were being asked to treat as meaningless something that they felt to be meaningful. The boss who expects sexual favours as a condition of promotion, or the date who expects a woman to 'put out' when he pays for dinner, are both more than willing to accept the principle of sexual disenchantment and thus view sex as a meaningless product to be exchanged on a free market ('You suck me off, I give you some good of equivalent value'). One student wrote, for instance, of hooking up with one of her peers:

> He slid inside me and I didn't say a word. At the time, I didn't know why. Maybe I didn't want to feel like I'd led him on. Maybe I didn't want to disappoint him. Maybe I just didn't want to deal with the 'let's do it, but no, we shouldn't' verbal tug-of-war that so often happens before sleeping with someone. It was easier to just do it. Besides, we were already in bed, and this is what people in bed do. I felt an obligation, a duty to go through with it. I felt guilty for not wanting to. I wasn't a virgin. I'd done this before. It shouldn't have been a big deal – *it's just sex* – so I didn't want to make it one.[24]

'It's just sex' summarises the sexual disenchantment idea perfectly. This young woman wasn't beaten, she didn't get pregnant, and she actually quite liked the young man she had sex with, at least at first. So why did she experience this sexual encounter as such a big deal? Because sexual disenchantment isn't actually true, and we all know it, including the liberal feminists who expend so much energy on arguing, for instance, that 'sex work is work.' You can tell because, when it became clear that Harvey Weinstein had been offering women career opportunities in exchange for sexual favours, these same liberal feminists immediately condemned him – not only for the violence and threats he had used in the course of committing his crimes but also for requesting sexual favours from his subordinates in the first place.

There was an intuitive recognition that asking for sex from an employee is not at all the same as asking them to do overtime or make coffee. I've made plenty of coffees for various employers in the past, despite the fact that coffee-making wasn't included in my job description, and I'm sure most readers will have done the same. But, while it might sometimes be annoying to receive this request, no worker who makes coffee for their boss will expect to end up dependent on drugs or alcohol as a consequence. No one will expect to become pregnant or acquire a disease that causes infertility. No one will expect to suffer from PTSD or other mental illness. No one will expect to become incapable of having healthy intimate relationships for the rest of her life. Everyone knows that having sex is not the same as making coffee, and when an ideology of sexual disenchantment demands that we pretend otherwise the result can be a distressing form of cognitive dissonance.

And liberal feminists don't have the conceptual framework necessary to resolve this distress. *The Guardian*'s Jessica Valenti, for instance, described the phenomenon of violating sex that doesn't actually meet the legal threshold for rape in a column written at the height of Me Too: 'It's true that women are fed up with sexual violence and harassment; but it's also true that what this culture considers "normal" sexual behavior is often harmful to women, and that we want that to stop, too.'[25]

But an anthology of essays on the subject of Me Too, edited by Valenti and published in 2020, demonstrates the inability of her brand of liberal feminism to respond properly to the problem she identifies.[26] The contributors to the anthology all want sexual violence to end, and rightly so. But they're queasy about using the power of the state to arrest and imprison rapists, and they don't want women to have to change their behaviour in order to avoid exposure to dangerous men, since even raising this possibility is regarded as 'victim blaming'.

Rather than propose alternatives – vigilante justice, anyone? – the writers avoid contending with difficult questions at all. They limit themselves to milquetoast ideas such as helping men to overcome their 'masculine insecurities' (Tahir Duckett) or creating community spaces in which perpetrators can seek 'healing and justice' (Sarah Deer and Bonnie Clairmont). Contributors such as the campaigner Andrea L. Pino-Silva write of the need to 'talk seriously about ending sexual violence' but propose nothing more concrete than workshops on university campuses that, among much else, 'celebrate and empower queerness'. Pino-Silva believes that such workshops won't work unless they also tackle every form of oppression under the sun, from colonialism to biphobia. I don't believe these workshops will work at all, so I suppose that's one point we can agree on.

Some contributors not only reject ideas that might go some way towards alleviating the problem of sexual violence, they actually propose ideas that will *make the problem worse*. Sassafras Lowrey encourages rape survivors to seek out sexual partners with a taste for violence, otherwise known as 'joining the BDSM community', and Tina Horn presents prostitution as a benign career route for young women. This is the central principle of liberal feminism taken to its logical conclusion: a woman should be able to do anything she likes, whether that be selling sex or inviting consensual sexual violence, since all of her desires and choices must necessarily be good, no matter where they come from or where they lead. And if anything bad comes from following this principle, then we return to the only solution that liberal feminism has to offer: 'teach men not to rape.'

But then what else can liberal feminists advise? They have made the error of buying into an ideology that has always best served the likes of Hugh Hefner and Harvey Weinstein, his true heir. And from this they derive the false belief that women are still suffering only because the sexual liberation project of the 1960s is unfinished, rather than because it was always inherently flawed. Thus they prescribe more and more freedom and are continually surprised when their prescription doesn't cure the disease.

This fact becomes clear when we look at the twenty-first-century university campus, where the gospel of sexual liberation is preached loudest and where BDSM societies[27] and 'Sex Weeks'[28] are the new normal.[29] At the beginning of term, freshers are given a lecture on the importance of consent and sent on their way with 'I heart consent' badges and tote bags. The rule they're taught is simple enough: with consent, anything goes. And yet this simple rule is broken again and again, both through rape and through the more subtle forms of coercion that so many women recounted during Me Too. Few liberal feminists are willing to draw the link between the culture of sexual hedonism they promote and the anxieties over campus rape that have emerged at exactly the same time.

If they did, they might be forced to recognise that they have done a terrible thing in advising inexperienced young women to seek out situations in which they are alone and drunk with horny men who are not only bigger and stronger than they are but are also likely to have been raised on the kind of porn that normalises aggression, coercion and pain. But in liberal feminist circles you're not supposed to talk about the influence of online porn, or BDSM, or hook-up culture, or any of the other malign elements of our new sexual culture, because to do so would be to question the doctrine of sexual freedom. So young women are forced to learn for themselves that freedom has costs, and they are forced to learn the hard way, every time.

Chronological snobbery

This book began as a standard piece of cultural analysis, but I realised when I began writing that it needed to go further. It wasn't enough just to point out the problems with our new sexual culture and leave it at that – I needed to offer readers some real guidance on how to live. Advice on sex is too often trivialised and shoved to the back of the magazine, with feminist arguments over sexual culture dismissed as so much girly bickering. But what we're concerned with here is not only the most important relationships in most people's lives but also the continuation of our species. So when I chose the title of this chapter, I was thinking not only of the problem of sexual disenchantment but also of the role of the advice columnist, who is rarely taken as seriously as she should be. *Having* sex should be taken seriously, and so should *talking* about it. It's a serious matter.

The advice I'm offering applies almost exclusively to heterosexuals, particularly heterosexual women, because the effect of the sexual revolution on relations between the sexes is the subject of this book. And none of it is ground-breaking: anyone who has spent enough time living in the world and learning from her mistakes should be able to cobble together a set of rules that look much like mine. But while a lot of my advice will seem like common sense to most older readers, my experience of talking face-to-face with men and women under the age of thirty is that it is shocking enough to make a person's jaw drop (literally, in several cases).

I would probably have been just as shocked a decade ago, because I didn't know any of this when I was a younger woman.

I thought, stupidly, that I understood life better than anyone else, as teenagers typically do, and I realised my mistake only years later, having learned the hard way and having watched my friends do the same. This wasn't because my parents or other adults in my life failed me – far from it – and I wasn't in any way unusual among my peers. But I was raised in a liberal environment that leant too heavily on a simplistic 'progress' narrative of history, and the problem with this narrative is that it encourages us to ignore both the ways in which things may have become worse over time and the advice offered by older generations. C. S. Lewis coined the phrase 'chronological snobbery' to describe '[T]he uncritical acceptance of the intellectual climate of our own age and the assumption that whatever has gone out of date is on that count discredited.'[30]

Older people are dismissed by snobbish twenty-first-century liberals as not only foolish and uninteresting but also (far worse) as 'problematic'. While in most cultures the elderly are regarded as sources of wisdom, and thus granted particular respect, in the modern West they are more likely to be disregarded and condescended to, shut away in nursing homes and assumed to be of no use to anyone.

At the end of every year, a rush of articles in liberal publications advise twenty-somethings on how best to withstand the problematic opinions voiced by older relatives over Thanksgiving or Christmas dinner ('It's your responsibility to challenge bigoted relatives over the holidays', advised *Teen Vogue*, for instance, in 2019). The fetishisation of youth in our culture has given us the false idea that it is young people who are best placed to provide moral guidance to their elders, despite their obvious lack of experience. And for anyone nudging forty, be assured that the 'problematic' bell also tolls for thee. The articles that have appeared regularly since 2018 on the 'homophobia, sexism and fat-shaming' in the sitcom *Friends* prove the need for constant renewal within the progress model.[31] When popular culture less than three decades old is already condemned as unacceptable, what hope have *people* who are more than three decades old of keeping pace? They can't, that's the point – the model demands that we reject them.

Within living memory, we have witnessed a very sudden break with the norms of the past, and the necessity of this break is constantly justified in the liberal media through reference to the bad old days. This kind of present-centrism is parodied beautifully in a 2020 TV adaptation of Aldous Huxley's *Brave New World* in which the 'Savage Lands' – more like an Indian reservation in the novel – are reimagined as a theme park devoted to twenty-first-century American decline. Twenty-sixth-century New London visitors load onto a tour bus and gawp at the 'house of correction' (a prison) and the 'house of monogamy' (a church), and witness a re-enactment of what is presented as the most important event in the savages' calendar, 'the annual day of black' (Black Friday), in which shoppers tear each other to pieces in their lust for bargains.

A tour guide informs visitors cheerfully that the key elements of savage culture included 'jealousy, competition, greed and strife.' She's not wrong, of course. The Savage Lands theme park is designed to demonstrate to New Londoners the perils of the old way of life, and its inclusion in the drama is designed to show us how tempting the twenty-sixth century could seem when set beside the twenty-first. These future people have successfully rid themselves of many of our flaws: their lack of privacy ensures a lack of crime; their lack of family ensures a lack of in-group preference; and their lack of monogamy ensures a lack of sexual jealousy. The cost that citizens pay for all this stability is that they must live under an authoritarian regime that suppresses any discontent with the pleasure drug soma. This regime encourages the citizens of New London to visit the Savage Lands theme park because demonising the past serves to justify the status quo. Conservatives in our own era who *idealise* the past achieve much the same effect in reverse, because the past is a political weapon that can readily be used to colour our perspective on the present.

I reject the poisonous dichotomy that insists that the past must be either all good or all bad. I don't think that we should imitate any sexual culture of the past, but nor do I think that what we have seen over the last sixty years has been a process of relentless improvement. What's clever about the Savage Lands of *Brave New World* is that the theme park representation is honest, up to a point. The twenty-first century is an era of 'jealousy, competition, greed and strife' that is easy enough to condemn. But there is also a dishonest side to the Savage Lands, in that highlighting the evils of the past also serves to distract from the evils of the present. Today's progressive representation of life in the 1950s serves much the same purpose.

In 2016, an extract from a 1950s home economics book offering 'tips to look after your husband' went viral on social media. The housewife was advised that, when her husband got home from work, she should have dinner on the table, her apron off and a ribbon in her hair, and that she should always make sure to let her husband 'talk first'.[32] This advice was not unusual for housewife manuals of the time, or indeed those of earlier eras, all of which advise women to make their housekeeping look effortless, hiding grime and exertion from their menfolk.

How reactionary, we think now, how stupid and backward! But then take a look at a small sample of *Cosmopolitan* magazine guides published within the last decade: '30 ways to please a man',[33] '20 ways to turn on your man',[34] or 'How to turn him on – 42 things to do with a naked man'[35] (this last guide includes 'rim him' and 'dole out some flavored lube'). In what sense are these guides not encouraging precisely the same degree of focus on male desires, except in this case it is sexual pleasure rather than domestic comfort? The only difference I can see is that the arse licking is now literal.

Women are still expected to please men and to make it look effortless. But while the 1950s 'angel of the house' hid her apron, the modern 'angel of the bedroom' hides her pubic hair. This waxed and willing swan glides across the water, concealing the fact that beneath the surface she is furiously working to maintain her image of perfection. She pretends to orgasm, pretends to like anal sex, and pretends not to mind when the 'friends with benefits' arrangement causes her pain. I've spoken to women who suffered from vaginismus for years without telling their partners that being penetrated was excruciating. I've also spoken to women who have had abortions after hook-ups and never told the men who impregnated them because, while sharing the inside of their bodies was expected, revealing the inconvenient fact of their fertility felt too intimate. We have smoothly transitioned from one form of feminine subservience to another, but we pretend that this one is liberation.

This pretence hurts the Marilyn Monroes, particularly when they are poor and friendless, and I want above all in this book to speak to the young women who have been lied to by liberal feminism and so risk following a very, very dangerous example.

But the would-be Hugh Hefners are also hurt by the pretence, albeit in a less obvious way. Mouldering away in the Playboy mansion doesn't kill a person, but it does corrode them. True happiness is not to be found on a soiled mattress being ridden by a woman who doesn't even like you.

Liberal ideology flatters us by telling us that our desires are good and that we can find meaning in satisfying them, whatever the cost. But the lie of this flattery should be obvious to anyone who has ever realised after the fact that they were wrong to desire something, and hurt themselves, or hurt other people, in pursuing it. So I am going to propose an alternative form of sexual culture – one that recognises other human beings as real people, invested with real value and dignity. It's time for a sexual counter-revolution.

2

Men and Women Are Different

A Natural History of Rape by Randy Thornhill and Craig T. Palmer is not a book that feminists are supposed to like.[1] It isn't even a book that feminists are supposed to read. Following its publication in 2000, the authors of this academic book were widely denounced in the media and for a while received so many credible death threats that they were advised by the police to check their cars for bombs regularly.[2] Thornhill and Palmer's efforts to offer an evolutionary explanation for rape were not – to put it mildly – generally well received.

But when I first came across the book, I read it compulsively, all in one sitting, and was left by the end feeling both disconsolate and oddly satisfied. I was working at the time at a rape crisis centre. My job was to work one-to-one with women and girls who had been raped, but I also had a teaching role, training volunteers for our helpline and going into schools to teach consent workshops. The ideology that I was expected to teach leant heavily on a very particular academic model of rape, and over time I had developed doubts about this model. *A Natural History of Rape* was a revelation to me because it articulated those doubts and gave them substance. I learned that I hadn't been wrong to think that there was a problem with the conventional feminist understanding of rape – the problem really was there, and it couldn't be wished away.

The 1975 book *Against Our Will* by Susan Brownmiller remains the foundational feminist text on the subject of rape. Indeed, it has become a classic, so much so that in 1995 it was selected by the New York Public Library as one of 100 most important books of the twentieth century.[3] Its fame is deserved, since Brownmiller's analysis was revolutionary, if flawed, and arrived at a crucial historical moment during the height of the feminist second wave. In particular, Brownmiller's claim that rape has historically more often been conceptualised as a property crime committed against a woman's male kin rather than as a crime committed against the woman herself was both true and timely. This is why marital rape – the abuse of a husband's 'property' – was only relatively recently criminalised in the West, and it remains legal in many non-Western countries. The fight for its criminalisation has been one of the great feminist campaigning efforts of the last century and has not yet been fully won. *Against Our Will* helped to galvanise that effort in the 1970s and 1980s, which was a very fine achievement. For that alone, the book merits praise.

Brownmiller's argument is summed up in a famous quote from *Against Our Will*, in which she describes rape as 'nothing more or less than a conscious process of intimidation by which *all* men keep *all* women in a state of fear.'[4] Brownmiller's model understands rape as an expression of political, as well as physical, dominance. Thus she suggests that the vast over-representation of men among perpetrators of rape is a product not of biology but, rather, of patriarchy: a social system which privileges male interests over female ones. According to this view, rapists are not born but made – they are the products of a culture that encourages men to see women as their sexual playthings. And so, to end rape, we must first end patriarchy.

Over the last fifty years, this argument has remained influential among feminists of every ideological persuasion.

For instance Jill Filipovic, writing in *The Guardian* in 2013, expresses a mainstream feminist idea when she insists that rape is 'about both power and violence. Rapists use sex organs as the locus of their violence, but rape isn't about sex, at least not in the sense of being motivated by sexual attraction or an uncontrollable sexual urge.'[5] This sentiment is often expressed in one, succinct phrase: 'rape is about power, not sex.'

I often repeated this view as a rape crisis worker – in fact, I probably used the exact phrase. I felt that to say otherwise – to suggest that rapists are motivated by sexual desire, not just a desire for control – would be to excuse them, which of course I didn't want to do, given that I was daily witnessing the terrible and lasting harm done by rape. Plus there really is some truth to the claim – workplace sexual harassment, for instance, is almost never perpetrated by junior men against more senior women. Instead it follows a predictable gradient: perpetrated by those with more power against those with less.

But I realise now that I wanted to believe that power was the whole story in large part because I found the alternative hypothesis too depressing for words. In a new preface to *Against Our Will*, written in 2013, Brownmiller (ungenerously) represented this alternative:

> Some evolutionary biologists believe quite strongly in the grim inevitability of 'men will be men.' A vocal handful of neo-Darwinians theorize that rape is a cost-effective strategy for males (embedded with drives for aggression, promiscuity, and reproduction) to spread their genes widely with a minimal amount of parental investment. What a fancy argument for rape, and for the failure to pay child support, as natural behavior![6]

If we think that rape is 'natural behaviour' then we must – according to Brownmiller's view here – also think of it as, firstly, permissible and, secondly, inevitable. This first claim is a textbook example of the naturalistic fallacy: the false belief that because something is natural it must necessarily be good. But the second claim is more difficult. If rape is indeed a product of evolution, does that make it inevitable? Well, not necessarily, but it certainly does make it more difficult to eradicate, which is, I think, a key reason for the historical reluctance of feminists to accept the scientific argument that Brownmiller is so contemptuous of. Instead, most feminists continue to favour socialisation theory as the preferred way of explaining male and female behaviour, both good and bad. This theory is popular among liberal feminists, whom I discussed at length in the last chapter, but it is also popular among the other key group of feminists still active in the twenty-first century: radical feminists, generally defined as those feminists who call for the radical restructuring of a society understood to be male supremacist.

Socialisation theory insists that there are no innate psychological differences between men and women, and that any differences we observe must be the product of nurture, not nature. There is some evidence in support of this theory. In her bestselling book *Delusions of Gender*, the Australian academic and author Cordelia Fine outlines the long history of researchers' attempts to find definitive proof for innate differences, concluding that the case for socialisation theory is ultimately much stronger. She makes clear that there is plenty of evidence that males and females experience very different treatment throughout their lifetimes. For instance, in one typical study described by Fine:

> Mothers were shown an adjustable sloping walkway, and asked to estimate the steepness of slope their crawling eleven-month-old child could manage and would attempt. Girls and boys differed in neither crawling ability nor risk taking when it came to testing them on the walkway. But mothers underestimated girls and over-estimated boys – both in crawling ability and

crawling attempts – meaning that in the real world they might often wrongly think their daughters incapable of performing or attempting some motor feats, and equally erroneously think their sons capable of others.[7]

These differences in socialisation start from the moment a child is born, and we don't know exactly how much of an effect they have long term. However, it seems likely that they do have *some* effect and that the observed psychological differences between the sexes are therefore at least partially attributable to childhood socialisation. Thus feminism in the post-second-wave era has often paid close attention to childrearing, for instance objecting to toys or advertising that promote gender stereotypes.

At the heart of this resocialisation project is a fundamentally utopian idea: if the differences we see between the sexes are entirely socialised, then they must also be entirely curable through cultural reform, which means that, if all of us, right now, could accept the feminist truth and start raising our children differently, then within a generation we could remake the world.

It's a nice idea, and I used to sincerely believe in it. But the evidence put forward by the authors of *A Natural History of Rape*, as well as many other scientists, forces us to reckon with a possibility that is a lot less appealing: what if it's not that easy? What if hierarchy, and viciousness, and violence are baked in? What if the feminist task is much, much harder than we've previously acknowledged?

Human animals

Brownmiller writes in *Against Our Will* that 'no zoologist, as far as I know, has ever observed that animals rape in their natural habitat, the wild.'[8] This statement is wrong – egregiously wrong, in fact, because plenty of other animals commit rape, and they also behave in all of the other horrible ways in which human beings sometimes behave. This grim fact has been revealed in many studies published within the last forty-seven years, but it was already well known by 1975. A few years earlier, for instance, the British primatologist John MacKinnon had published his pioneering account of fifteen and a half months spent observing wild orangutans and had described many instances of 'unwilling females being raped by aggressive males.'[9] Other researchers have since observed the same behaviour among orangutans,[10] as well as among other animals.[11] We are not the only species that rapes.

Socialisation theory depends upon a furtive form of human exceptionalism, by which we are understood to be both uniquely detached from the normal processes of natural selection and uniquely corruptible by cultural influence. We do bad things, according to this analysis, not because we are as fallible as any other animal, but because we have *chosen* to invent cultures that corrupt innocent little babies and turn them to wickedness. This 'blank slate' view gives ultimate authority to society in moulding the human character, for good and ill.

There is a more credible way of understanding the world, but it is one that offers much less scope for human perfectibility and so is much less appealing to utopians. Instead of unwittingly imitating the religious fundamentalists of the nineteenth century who resisted Darwin, we could instead understand human beings to be animals – more specifically, members of the Hominidae, the Great Apes, a taxonomic family of primates that includes seven other extant species. As the feminist and evolutionary biologist Sarah Blaffer Hrdy writes:

> We are not ready-made out of somebody's rib. We are composites of many different legacies, put together from leftovers in an evolutionary process that has been going on for billions of years.

Even the endorphins that made my labor pains tolerable came from molecules that humans still share with earthworms.[12]

As a consequence of these many different legacies, coupled with evolutionary selection pressures favouring these traits, we sometimes demonstrate kindness, gentleness and friendliness. At other times we kill, torture and rape. And, like other hominids, male and female members of our species are different in certain important ways – both physiologically and behaviourally.

Let's start with some of the physiological differences. Adult women are approximately half as strong as adult men in the upper body and two-thirds as strong in the lower body.[13] On average, men can bench press more mass than women can by a factor of roughly two and a half[14] and can punch harder by a similar factor.[15] In hand grip strength, 90 per cent of females produce less force than 95 per cent of males.[16] In other words, almost all women are weaker than almost all men, and any feminist analysis of the power dynamic between men and women has to begin with the recognition of this fact.

And men can out-run women, as well as out-punch them. Sex differences are less marked in sports that favour endurance rather than strength alone, but they are nevertheless considerable. In Olympic swimming and track events, women's performances hover at around 90 per cent of men's, a figure sometimes referred to as the 'golden ratio' of athletics.[17] This may sound minor, but it translates into stunning differences at the upper end of the distribution, where elite athletes are to be found. At the 2016 summer Olympics, for instance, Elaine Thompson of Jamaica won gold with a time of 10.71 seconds. In the same games, Usain Bolt, also of Jamaica, won with a time of 9.81 seconds. Although there was less than a second's difference between these two athletes, if men and women had been running in the same event, then Thompson wouldn't even have made it into the final race. In fact, she would have been easily out-run by Jamaican boys competing in the under-seventeen category,[18] just as the United States women's national football team in 2017 were beaten by the Dallas under-fifteen boys' team,[19] composed of boys who had just crossed the crucial puberty line and so had begun to develop the strength and power of adult men. The women's category has traditionally been protected in elite sports because, if it were not protected, there would be no women in elite sports – men would out-compete them every time.

For most people this observation is common sense, particularly those who have any experience of competing in sports or even just play fighting with siblings of the opposite sex. In the twenty-first century, the only group pushing back against the fact of physical differences between the sexes are liberal feminists, some of whom suggest that the women's category in sports should be opened to trans athletes who have transitioned from male to female and have undergone some degree of medical intervention to reverse the effects of male puberty. Some liberal feminists go even further, arguing that the women's category ought to be dissolved altogether. The British feminist Laurie Penny, for instance, wrote in 2016 on the controversy over the inclusion of trans athletes in that year's summer Olympics: 'Strict gender segregation is seldom questioned, which conveniently allows women's events to be sidelined while ensuring that no sportsman will ever be beaten by a woman. But dividing sports by gender isn't natural or inevitable.'[20]

Female athletes including Paula Radcliffe, Sharron Davies and Kelly Holmes – for whom sex differences are more than a merely philosophical problem – have strongly objected to this idea,[21] with Davies, for instance, insisting that, '[in order] to protect women's sport, those with a male sex advantage should not be able to compete in women's sport.'[22] Contrary to Penny's claims, no sportsman wants to maintain sex segregation in sport because he's afraid of being beaten by a woman

– anyone with any practical experience of sport knows that such a fear would be fanciful.

But recognising these kinds of physical limitation does not sit well with a liberal feminist project that aims to challenge any restrictions on human freedom. If we acknowledge that there are immovable differences between the sexes in terms of strength and speed, then we are also forced to acknowledge not only that natal males cannot fairly compete in women's sports, but also that natal females experience a permanent physical disadvantage. And the consequences of this disadvantage go well beyond sports, particularly when male upper body strength is set beside the fragility of the female throat and skull. In the modern West, it has become increasingly possible to become detached from the sexually dimorphic body when one does not do a manual job, compete in sports or bear children. But the unwelcome truth will always remain, whether or not we can bear to look at it: almost all men can kill almost all women with their bare hands, but not vice versa. And that matters.

Differences above the neck

In contrast to their liberal counterparts, radical feminists are fully willing to accept the fact of innate physical differences between the sexes. Conventionally, however, neither liberals nor radicals are willing to go a step further and accept an even more difficult fact – that there are also innate differences 'above the neck'. Radical feminists committed to socialisation theory can acknowledge the *existence* of male upper body strength, but they refuse to acknowledge its *cause*.

The growth of broad, muscly shoulders in boys costs the body energy that could be spent on other natural processes. This tells us that, during our evolutionary history, boys who developed strong upper bodies experienced a selection advantage. In the present day, we know that men with heavily muscled upper bodies are considered more attractive to straight women from a wide range of cultural backgrounds,[23] and we also know that men with this body type have a fighting advantage – both against other animals and against other men. It is impossible to explain this fact unless we recognise that fighting must have played an important role in men's evolutionary history, which also obliges us to recognise that sex-specific behaviour must also have been subject to natural selection.

But we often run into difficulties when we try to apply this insight to the real world, because readers sceptical of the evolutionary account of gendered behaviour will probably be thinking right now about individual men they know who don't have especially broad shoulders and have never shown any interest in fighting of any kind. It's very easy to hear 'men and women are *on average* a certain way' and understand this to mean 'men and women are *always like this*', which anyone with any experience of the world will know is not true. There are lots of men and women who are physically dissimilar from other members of their sex, and very many more who don't fit masculine or feminine stereotypes in terms of their interests and behaviour. In fact, I'd go further, and suggest that almost no one is a walking gender stereotype – I have some stereotypically feminine traits and some stereotypically masculine ones, and I'm sure you do too.

But this kind of anecdotal evidence does not disprove the claim that there are some important average differences between the sexes, and that at the population level these differences have an effect. We can insist simultaneously that there are plenty of exceptions to the rule, and moreover that there is *nothing wrong* with being an exception to the rule, while also acknowledging the existence of the rule.

We are a sexually dimorphic species, but not quite as sexually dimorphic as some others. For instance, the male northern elephant seal, found in the eastern Pacific Ocean, is three times heavier than the female, and these males and females also have strikingly different behaviour patterns in terms of diet and migration. Not coincidentally, this species is also highly polygynous, with a single male inseminating as many as fifty females in a mating season. In contrast, the male harbour seal, found along Arctic and European coasts, is almost the same weight as the female and is mostly monogamous, with males and females demonstrating similar behaviour. We are closer to harbour seals than we are to elephant seals, since our females weigh on average just 25 per cent less than our males and most of our societies are only mildly polygynous. But there is some degree of sexual dimorphism that, while it may be tempered by cultural conditions, remains evident in every human society.

The complication is that we are in one particular way different from harbour seals and northern elephant seals: as a species, we are uniquely intelligent. This means that, unlike other animals, we can choose to defy our instincts, at least to some extent, and, also unlike other animals, we have been able to spread ourselves across the planet and adjust to a wide range of environments. This kind of variation in material conditions can sometimes cause human societies to develop in very different directions. For instance, in a few cultures, mating customs look strange to us. The Na in China are famous for having no institution of marriage and deliberately suppressing long-term pair bonding, and a few Amazonian groups believe that a child can have two or more biological fathers. The anomalous mating customs of the twenty-first-century West – the subject of this book – are the product not of climate or terrain but, rather, of new technologies not available to people in the past, as I argued in chapter 1.

But all of this variation is built upon a biological substrate. Liberal feminists and trans activists may do their best to deny this, but it is still true that only one half of the human race is capable of getting pregnant, and – failing the invention of artificial wombs – this will remain true indefinitely. What's more, even if we were somehow to remove the human body entirely from reproduction, we would still be left with our human brains, which remain the products of our evolution. Natural selection has not kept pace with rapid social change. The brains we have now are little different from the brains of our nineteenth-century ancestors, or indeed those of our hunter gatherer ancestors, since hunting and gathering was humanity's first and most successful adaptation, occupying at least 90 per cent of human history.

The effect of natural selection on psychological differences between men and women is politically thorny for a very good reason – it can easily be misused. Evolutionary psychologists are sometimes accused by their critics of telling Just So Stories that sound intuitively convincing but have no real evidence behind them, and there is some truth to this accusation. Some amateur theorists, and even some professionals, have run riot with their imaginations, and it is, sadly, the anti-feminists who have proved to be the most provocatively imaginative.

An unfortunate effect of the feminist rejection of evolutionary psychology is that most feminists have deliberately stepped away from the discipline and so played only a minor role in shaping it. In fact, the *very idea* of there being evolved psychological differences between the sexes has become so taboo in some circles that even voicing the possibility is taken to be an indication of anti-feminist sentiment. In 2017, Google engineer James Damore circulated an internal memo in which he suggested that the under-representation of women at Google might partly be a consequence of (in his words) 'differences in distributions of traits between men and women'.[24] The scientific research that Damore cited was perfectly sound, but he was nevertheless fired for violating Google's code of conduct, provoking a media storm.

The result of the taboo is that the people willing publicly to support the evolutionary account often fall into one of two categories – either they are not sensitive to the existence of the taboo (Damore, being autistic, was probably in this category),[25] or they are genuinely anti-feminist. It is telling that so many of the lay enthusiasts for evolutionary psychology tend to focus on one particular issue, sometimes obsessively: affirmative action designed to increase the representation of women in STEM. Part of the backlash against Damore was a result of the fact that women who work at male-dominated organisations such as Google often experience everyday sexist insults that range from mild condescension to outright sexual harassment, and many have therefore quite legitimately become sensitive to clumsy talk of 'male brains' and 'female brains' that can provide cover for claims of female inferiority.

I happen to agree with Damore that the under-representation of women in STEM is probably partly attributable to innate biological differences, but that, as Damore wrote in his original memo, 'many of these differences are small and there's significant overlap between men and women, so you can't say anything about an individual given these population level distributions.'[26] What we're talking about when it comes to interest in the highly specialised world of tech is two bell curves that overlap, and, just as in endurance sports, it's only at the tails that any average difference becomes obvious.

But while sex differences in STEM are no doubt important to people who work in those fields, in the great scheme of things they are a sideshow. There are some much bigger and more important psychological differences between the sexes that deserve our urgent attention, but what I often find when I speak to a certain kind of male enthusiast for evolutionary psychology is that they are not interested in discussing these issues. I say that I think Damore was unfairly treated and they nod along happily. But when I raise the issue of male violence they are suddenly nowhere to be seen, since this issue casts men in a rather less flattering light.

Or, worse, they fall prey to the naturalistic fallacy. In 2020, Will Knowland, an English teacher at Eton College – the oldest and poshest school in the UK – attracted a great deal of media attention when he was dismissed for producing a video titled 'The Patriarchy Paradox' as part of a course on critical thinking intended for older students.[27] Knowland later alleged that he was disciplined because 'the Head Master felt that some of the ideas put forward in my lecture – such as the view that men and women differ psychologically and not all of those differences are socially constructed – were too dangerous for the boys to be exposed to.'[28] I've no doubt this was indeed why Knowland fell foul of the authorities at Eton, at least in part, but while I am sympathetic to James Damore, given his treatment by Google, I am not sympathetic to Knowland. Some of his claims are straightforwardly false, and he betrays a poor understanding of feminism, for instance using the term 'radical feminism' to mean 'extreme feminism' (always a giveaway). And while his video covers some of the same ground that I have covered in this chapter, for instance strength and aggression differences between men and women, Knowland uses evolutionary biology to argue both that women are inherently inferior to men (not only smaller and weaker but also less creative and innovative), and that men have been uniquely victimised throughout human history, while women have been coddled.

I fully understand why so many feminists are repulsed by any association with the ideology of anti-feminists such as Knowland. But we should not respond to the misuse of a scientific discipline by rejecting that discipline altogether. The evidence itself is morally neutral and can be put to all sorts of political purposes, even feminist ones. *A Natural History of Rape* hit me like a ton of bricks because it alerted me to the feminist potential of evolutionary psychology, a discipline I had previously rejected as inherently suspect.

Rape as adaptation

I wrote in chapter 1 that the central feminist question ought not to be 'How can we all be free?' but, rather, 'How can we best promote the wellbeing of both men and women, given that these two groups have different sets of interests, which are sometimes in tension?' Evolutionary psychology draws attention to the ways in which men and women's interests are in tension, which makes the discipline difficult to reconcile with a liberal feminist emphasis on freedom or a radical feminist emphasis on utopianism. But if we stop aiming for either absolute freedom or utopia, and start thinking more pragmatically about how best to protect women's interests in the here and now, then we can start to reconceptualise evolutionary psychology as a useful tool.

I sought out *A Natural History of Rape* because I was bothered by certain questions that socialisation theory couldn't answer – why, for instance, such a high proportion of rape victims are teenagers. My own experience of working with victims had given me a glimpse of the demographics, and more systematic research confirms what I suspected to be the case: there is a very obvious peak in female victimisation, with the risk increasing very rapidly after the age of about twelve and decreasing again, almost as rapidly, after the age of about thirty. The very young and the very old are sometimes targeted, but this is rare: the modal victim is fifteen,[29] and the percentage of female victims who are older than thirty when they are raped is in single digits.[30] Could it really be a coincidence, I wondered, that the age of peak rape victimisation is also the age at which I personally attracted the most sexual harassment on the street? It turns out this isn't a coincidence, as the sociologists Richard Felson and Richard Moran write:

> Social science has demonstrated a strong relationship between age and sexual attractiveness. Heterosexual men are sexually

attracted to young women, while homosexual men are attracted to young men. The age preference explains why adult film stars, sex workers, exotic dancers as well as glamour models are often young, and why their earnings decline as they age.[31]

Female rape victimisation and female sexual attractiveness peak at exactly the same age – the two graphs map onto each other almost perfectly. Socialisation theory can't account for this because, if 'rape is about power, not sex', why would rapists just happen to target the age group that also just happens to be the most sexually desirable to men?

And then there's the age of the rapists themselves. This skew isn't quite as extreme as it is among female victims, but there is still a very clear peak among young men: one typical study found 46 per cent of rapists to be under age twenty-five, 17 per cent under age eighteen, and 15 per cent under age fifteen.[32] This fits not only with the age profile of violent offenders in general – who are overwhelmingly young men – but also with the peak of male sex drive.[33] Again, if 'rape is about power, not sex', why would this be the case?

There was another issue I had been having doubts about when I first opened *A Natural History of Rape*. In victim surveys, the proportion of rape victims who are male is typically somewhere between 2 and 5 per cent, with almost all of these rapes committed by other men. It had occurred to me, while looking over the data, that this is about the same proportion of the male population that identifies as gay or bisexual – a coincidence, according to the Brownmiller model, but highly suggestive if we move beyond it, given that gay and bisexual men commit rape about as often as straight men do, but the victims of these rapists, of course, include other men and boys. Given this, should we still understand rape to be an expression of political dominance rooted in patriarchy, or should we instead consider a much more obvious possibility: that rape is an aggressive expression of sexual desire?

Resistance to this research evidence comes from two very different groups, both of whom tend either to ignore the data or quibble with it, and often end up – perversely – echoing each other. The first is anti-feminist men's rights activists, and the second is those feminists who, in an effort to be as inclusive as possible, deliberately avoid making any generalisations about either rapists or their victims. While teaching workshops, a rape crisis colleague, for instance, used to use the phrase 'people of all genders sexually assault people of all genders' – a statement that is technically true, in the sense that you can find examples of every possible configuration of victim and perpetrator, but is misleading in its framing.

In every part of the world, something in the region of 98 to 99 per cent of convicted sex offenders are male, and the women who make up the remaining 1 to 2 per cent typically offend quite differently. For instance, women are much more likely to offend alongside a male co-offender (usually a husband or boyfriend), and women almost never assault strangers. This is not to say that there are zero examples of women committing stranger rape or other male-typical crimes – in a world containing more than 7 billion people, rare events happen every day – but it is foolish to the point of dishonesty to pretend that there is not a very obvious pattern at play here.

No, I'm afraid that rape is a male crime, and not only in our species but also in many others. And it has evolved for a startlingly obvious reason: as Wrangham and Peterson put it, 'rape has entered some species' behavioural repertoire because it can increase an individual male's success in passing on genes to the next generation (as all evolved behaviours ultimately must).'[34] In other words, it is one method by which males can reproduce – it confers, in some situations, a selection advantage.

This is the central thesis of *A Natural History of Rape*, a book that applies evolutionary theory to the task of understanding the causes of rape and the best methods of preventing it.

We start from the recognition that reproduction places more physical demands on women than it does on men (sitting here writing this while six months pregnant, I can personally attest to this). Pregnancy lasts more than nine months and is followed by a dangerous labour, which is followed by many more years of breast-feeding and infant care. Men, however, really *need* to expend only the amount of effort it takes to orgasm in order to reproduce. It may also be advantageous for fathers to hang around after conception and increase the mother and baby's chances of survival, but it isn't always necessary: a man who can game the system by abandoning a woman after impregnating her, and then riding off into the sunset to impregnate many more women, is also successfully spreading his genetic material. He carries the risk of retribution, including violence from the woman's male kin, but in some instances the benefits may outweigh the risks. Put differently, there are different modes of male sexuality: the mode that encourages commitment and the mode that encourages promiscuity (much more on this in chapter 4).

When it was first published, *A Natural History of Rape* attracted a great deal of criticism from feminists, some of whom misrepresented the contents of the book.[35] Many critics misunderstood the argument that was being made or else refused to accept that Thornhill and Palmer were sincere in their condemnation of rape, despite the fact that the authors were at pains throughout the book to highlight the harm caused by rape and chose to dedicate the work to 'the women and girls in our lives'.

Too few of these feminist critics recognised how useful the book could be in designing policies that actually work to prevent rape, and indeed in thinking more broadly about how a sexual culture might impact men and women differently. I strongly believe that this hostility to evolutionary biology is a mistake, which is why, in the rest of this book, I'm regularly going to use the work of evolutionary biologists in the course of making feminist arguments – once we accept that men and women are different, many other things follow.

How to bear it

What proportion of men have the desire to rape? Not all, I'm happy to report, although the proportion is still disturbingly high, as the evolutionary biologist David Buss writes:

> Individual men differ in their proclivity toward rape. In one study, men were asked to imagine that they had the possibility of forcing sex on someone else against her will with no chance of getting caught, no chance that anyone would find out, no risk of disease, and no possibility of damage to their reputation. Thirty-five percent indicated that there was some likelihood that they would force sex on the woman under these conditions, although in most cases the likelihood was slight. In another study that used a similar method, 27 percent of the men indicated that there was some likelihood that they would force sex on a woman if there was no chance of getting caught. Although these percentages are alarmingly high, if taken at face value they also indicate that most men are not potential rapists.[36]

A smaller proportion of men admit to having actually committed rape, usually phrased in surveys as something like 'forced an unwilling partner into sex' – in the United States and the UK, this figure hovers at around 10 per cent. In her work, the social psychologist and domestic abuse expert Dina McMillan also uses the figure of 10 per cent[37] as a rough ballpark for the proportion of the male population that are reliably dangerous. There is a core minority who will be sexually aggressive in most circumstances and a larger minority who will be sexually aggressive in some circumstances. This still means, thankfully, that the majority of men are not potential rapists – the infamous #NotAllMen hashtag is actually true.

Unfortunately, it's not easy for potential victims to identify potential rapists. Thornhill and Palmer do point out that, as we'd expect, 'incarcerated rapists exhibit significantly more sexual arousal in response to depictions of sexual coercion involving physical force than men who have not been convicted of sex offences.'[38] And Buss adds that, in terms of personality, rapists tend to be more impulsive, hostile, disagreeable, promiscuous, hyper-masculine, and low in empathy compared with other men.[39] In other words, it is sometimes possible to spot rapists, or at least to make generalisations about them. But not always.

So, how to avoid them? Most feminists – both liberal and radical – dislike this question, and I do understand why. Every now and again, a police force will release some kind of campaign about rape prevention – in 2015, for instance, Sussex Police produced posters that advised women to stick together on nights out, to keep their friends safe[40] – and invariably these efforts invite a feminist backlash. The Sussex Police posters were met by a petition for their removal, with the feminist authors of the petition writing that 'the people who have the most power to prevent rape and sexual assault from happening are not friends or bystanders but rather the perpetrators of the crime – the rapists.'[41]

Which is true, of course it is! But here's the point: *rapists don't care what feminists have to say.* I sympathise with the feminist instinct to object to even the slightest suggestion of victim blaming, particularly by police, since police forces across the world invariably have tarnished histories, and there continue to be all sorts of problems with the criminal justice system, which is why I have spent most of my adult life campaigning to improve both the law on sexual violence and its implementation. But posters that say 'don't rape' will prevent precisely zero rapes, because rape is already illegal, and would-be rapists know that. We can scream 'don't rape' until we're blue in the face, and it won't make a blind bit of difference.

It has to be possible to say simultaneously that rape is reprehensible and that it is OK – in fact, *essential* – to offer advice that could help to reduce its incidence. I could hardly have more contempt for rapists – I joke with my friends that I want to market a range of tiny guillotines to deal with rapists in a very direct manner – and yet I'm exhausted by a feminist discourse that can't move beyond just saying over and over again that rape is bad. Yes, rape is bad. We know that. Now let's actually do something about it.

There are two ways of reducing rape. The first is to constrain would-be rapists, for instance by imprisoning them, and the second is to limit opportunities for them to act on their desires. Prosecution rates for sexual crimes are appallingly low in every part of the world – in the UK, less than 1 per cent of rapes result in a conviction – which is partly due to low reporting rates, partly due to failures within the criminal justice system, and partly due to the fact that it is inherently difficult to prosecute rape committed by anyone other than a stranger and against anyone other than a child. It's always going to be challenging to prove beyond reasonable doubt the presence or absence of consent, even in a perfect system, and we don't have one of those.

I would like convicted rapists to spend much longer in prison – their whole lives, if needs be – because I have very little faith in the effectiveness of sex offender rehabilitation programmes. One such programme, run in prisons in England and Wales for more than a decade, was actually found to *slightly increase* rates of reoffending.[42] My perspective on this is often condemned as 'carceral feminism' by those who favour the abolition of prisons and policing, typically on the grounds of racial justice. My response to this accusation is that the women and children who make up the vast majority of rape victims are disproportionately likely to be both poor and non-white. If wanting to protect these potential victims from violence makes me a 'carceral feminist', then I wear the label with pride.

The feminists who describe me as 'carceral' are able to present only one alternative to imprisonment: resocialisation, typically attempted through consent workshops for children and young adults. I've both designed and taught these workshops and I don't think they're entirely useless, because they can achieve two things: they can teach participants (including potential victims) what is and is not illegal, and they can offer schools or other institutions the opportunity to declare a zero tolerance attitude. If, for instance, a student is caught sharing revenge porn having attended an official consent workshop, he or she can't plausibly claim not to have known that this was both illegal and punishable by expulsion.

However, consent workshops are very unlikely to prevent rape, because rape is not caused by a lack of education. Hundreds of thousands of years of sexual violence – not only in our own species but also in many others – is not a consequence of some kind of misunderstanding, swiftly cleared up during a 45-minute workshop in which kids are told in words of one syllable not to rape one another. Nurture does have a role to play: as we'll see in chapter 5, for instance, there is good reason to believe that violent porn can intensify an existing arousal pattern. But putting one's faith in resocialisation is not only foolish but dangerous.

If we accept the evidence from evolutionary biology and move beyond the Brownmiller model, then we can understand that rapists are really just men who are aroused by violence, have poor impulse control, and are presented with a suitable victim and a suitable set of circumstances. Those circumstances can include a victim who is drunk, high, or otherwise vulnerable, the absence of witnesses, and no fear of any legal or social repercussions. Both women and men in the sex trade are spectacularly vulnerable (much more on this in later chapters).

And young women between the ages of about thirteen and twenty-five are the prime group likely to be targeted.

If you wanted to design the perfect environment for the would-be rapist, then you couldn't do much better than a party or nightclub filled with young women who are wearing high heels (limiting mobility) and drinking or taking drugs (limiting awareness). Is it appalling for a person even to contemplate assaulting these women? Yes. Does that moral statement provide any protection to these women whatsoever? No. I made this mistake many, many times as a young woman, and I understand the cultural pressure. But, while young women should feel free to get hammered with their girlfriends or highly trusted men, doing so among strange men will always be risky.

I think we all know this, just as we all know that it's risky for young women to hitch-hike, travel alone, or go back to a strange man's house. The sorry truth is that something in the region of 10 per cent of men pose a risk, and those men aren't always identifiable on first sight, or even after long acquaintance. So my advice to young women has to be this: avoid putting yourself in a situation where you are alone with a man you don't know or a man who gives you a bad feeling in your gut. He is almost certainly stronger and faster than you, which means that the only thing standing between you and rape is that man's self-control. I know full well that this advice doesn't protect against all forms of rape, including (but not limited to) incestuous rape, prison rape, child rape and marital rape. I wish I could offer some advice to protect against these atrocities, but I can't.

Other feminists can gnash their teeth all they like, accuse me of victim blaming, and insist that the burden should be on rapists, not their victims, to prevent rape. But they have no other solutions to offer, since feeble efforts at resocialisation don't actually work. What does sometimes work is a solution that is unreliable, unfair and painfully, painfully costly: to reduce the opportunities available to would-be rapists and to imprison those who either cannot or will not resist their aggressive sexual impulses. Because rape isn't only about power, it's also about sex.

3

Some Desires Are Bad

The American social psychologist Jonathan Haidt likes to invent scenarios that test our moral intuitions. He will ask research participants to listen to a story, give their opinion on it, and then explain their reasoning. Here is one such scenario: imagine a man goes to a supermarket and buys himself a whole dead chicken. He takes it home, has sex with it, and then eats it. No one else ever finds out. Did he do anything wrong?

Haidt has several other scenarios concerned with sexual ethics. Is it OK for a brother and sister to have sex, if they use multiple forms of contraception, and no one else knows about it? Or, to use a real scenario, is it OK for a man to consent to being eaten by another man for the purposes of sexual gratification?[1] He has found that participants' responses tend to be affected by their political allegiances. Social conservatives generally give swift, confident answers, because they are able to appeal to values such as sanctity and authority. For them, having sex with a dead chicken or a sibling obviously violates religious or traditionalist moral principles and is therefore unacceptable. End of story.

Liberals have more difficulty: they want to say that the acts are wrong, because they are instinctively disgusted by them, but the scenarios are designed to prevent any appeal to J. S. Mill's harm principle: 'The only purpose for which power can be rightfully exercised over any member of a civilised community, against his will, is to prevent harm to others.' In the chicken example, for instance, it is difficult to identify anyone who has been harmed by the man's behaviour, since the chicken, being dead, can't be harmed, and other people, being ignorant of the act, can't be harmed either. The man is simply exercising his sexual autonomy, which means that, as Haidt puts it, 'if your moral matrix is limited to the ethic of autonomy, then you're at high risk of being dumbfounded by this case.'

Not everyone is dumbfounded, though. The American anthropologist Gayle Rubin, for instance – a key figure in the academic discipline of Queer Theory, which emerged in the 1970s and 1980s – would, I imagine, be unbothered by the chicken scenario, just as she is unbothered by unusual sexual behaviour in general. As she writes:

> In Western culture, sex is taken all too seriously. A person is not considered immoral, is not sent to prison, and is not expelled from her or his family, for enjoying spicy cuisine. But an individual may go through all this and more for enjoying shoe leather. Ultimately, of what possible social significance is it if a person likes to masturbate over a shoe?[2]

Rubin is radical in her liberalism. She famously rejects the idea of 'good' or 'bad' sexual behaviour, interpreting such moralising as inherently oppressive. To her mind, sex does not need to involve either love or commitment, and it certainly needn't have any connection to marriage or reproduction. The only thing that matters to liberal feminists such as Rubin is whether or not all parties are able and willing to consent to a particular sex act. All other sexual morality must be discarded – indeed, one group that was influential early on in arguing for the destigmatisation of commercial sex made the point crystal clear with their choice of name: COYOTE, 'Call Off Your Old Tired Ethics'.

Rubin's Queer Theory owed a great debt to Michel Foucault's *History of Sexuality*, the first volume of which was published in 1978. And Foucault, in his turn, owed a great debt to Sigmund Freud's writing on sexual repression. This intellectual tradition is interpreted by its proponents as a progressive undermining of bourgeois sexual norms, which have historically functioned to keep people with unusual sexual interests either locked out of respectable society or else made permanently unhappy when they are forced to hide their authentic sexual selves. The famous slogan of the May 1968 student protests in Paris, 'Il est interdit d'interdire!' (It is forbidden to forbid), makes the point succinctly and has become remarkably mainstream in the decades since, jumbled up with the feminist attempt to free women from traditional sexual norms that restricted female agency and pleasure. Thus the cause of Foucault, Rubin, Freud, and womankind as a whole is assumed by liberal feminism to be one and the same: 'us' (the revolutionaries) against 'them' (the traditionalists). Liberté, Égalité, Sexualité!

But I want to suggest a different framing – a class struggle, but not between the revolutionaries and the traditionalists but between two very different classes of people, with two very different sets of interests.

The sexual free market

Critics of free market capitalism have correctly observed that, within a society riven by gross inequalities of wealth and power, the pleasures of freedom are not equally available to all. As the economic historian and socialist R. H. Tawney wrote in 1931:

> Equality implies the deliberate acceptance of social restraints upon individual expansion. It involves the prevention of

sensational extremes of wealth and power by public action for the public good. If liberty means, therefore, that every individual shall be free, according to his opportunities, to indulge without limit his appetite for either, it is clearly incompatible, not only with economic and social, but with civil and political, equality, which also prevent the strong exploiting to the full the advantages of their strength . . . freedom for the pike is death for the minnows.[3]

Of course the factory owner supports free marketisation, and of course his wage slave disagrees – the pike and the minnow have different economic interests. This is also true in the sexual marketplace, which was once strictly regulated but has now been made (mostly) free.

However, in this case, the classes are not the workers and the bourgeoisie but, rather, men and women – or, more precisely, the group of people who have done particularly well out of the free marketisation of sex are men high in the personality trait that psychologists call 'sociosexuality': the desire for sexual variety.

The psychologist David Schmitt describes the importance of sociosexuality:

Those who score relatively low on this dimension are said to possess a restricted sociosexual orientation – they tend toward monogamy, prolonged courtship, and heavy emotional investment in long-term relationships. Those residing at the high end of sociosexuality are considered more unrestricted in mating orientation, they tend toward promiscuity, are quick to have sex, and experience lower levels of romantic relationship closeness.[4]

In a study of male and female sociosexuality across forty-eight countries, Schmitt and his team found large sex differences to be 'a cultural universal', regardless of a nation's level of economic and social equality between the sexes. Although there is of course variation within the sexes, with some individual women high in sociosexuality and some individual men low in it, the two bell curves are substantially different. This difference is explained by what evolutionary biologists term 'parental investment theory' – put simply, women can produce offspring at a maximum rate of about one pregnancy per year, whereas promiscuous men can theoretically produce offspring every time they orgasm. Although there are some limited circumstances in which multiple short-term mating might be advantageous for women – in conditions of danger and scarcity, for instance, in which sex might be exchanged for resources and protection – in general, natural selection has favoured women who are choosy about their mates.

We see this play out in male and female sexual behaviour. The research is clear: we know that men, on average, prefer to have more sex and with a larger number of partners, that sex buyers are almost exclusively male, that men watch a lot more porn than women do, and that the vast majority of women, if given the option, prefer a committed relationship to casual sex. Sexual fetishes (also known as 'paraphilias') are also much more commonly found in men than in women and, although the cause of this difference is not well understood, men's greater average sociosexuality seems to be a factor.[5] All in all, the evidence demonstrates that the acts that have become much more socially acceptable over the last sixty years are acts that men are much more likely to enjoy. It is a good time to be a fetishist, a sex buyer, a porn user and a playboy – it is the highly sociosexual who have done best out of sexual liberalism, and these people are overwhelmingly male.

There have also been other beneficiaries of sexual liberalisation – most importantly, lesbian, gay and bisexual people, whose relationships are now, for the first time, not only decriminalised but also granted state recognition in many countries. The decline in homophobia across the West within the last century is truly remarkable. In 1983, fully half of respondents told the British Social Attitudes Survey that 'sexual relations between adults of the same sex' were 'always wrong'.[6] By 2012, this proportion had more than halved, and, a year later, legislation introducing same-sex marriage in England and Wales was passed under a Conservative government. Since 2001, dozens of other countries have legalised same-sex marriage, including the United States in 2015[7] – a prospect that was almost unthinkable at the height of the AIDS crisis in 1989, when Andrew Sullivan was the first to make the case for this reform in a prominent American publication.[8]

Any historical event as radical as the sexual revolution is going to have a diverse range of effects, both positive and negative, but the key point I want to stress in this book is that it is wrong to interpret this historical period as an example of 'progress' in any straightforward sense. I am a 'progress' apostate: I do not believe that there is any such thing as the gradual, inevitable marching towards the good that Martin Luther King Junior so famously described as the 'arc of the moral universe' bending towards justice. Every social change has trade-offs, which are obscured by a simplistic narrative that leaves no space for complexity.

Sex is relational. This means, of course, that the loving partner needs another loving partner. But this also means that the fetishist with a taste for sadomasochism, voyeurism or dirty underwear needs other people to participate in his fetish, just as the sex buyer needs sex sellers and the porn user needs porn producers. This isn't a problem for a theorist such as Gayle Rubin, who would point out that plenty of people (mostly, by necessity, women) are available to provide for these desires – sometimes readily, sometimes in return for financial compensation. But this underestimates the extent to which participants in the sexual free market may be subjected to more or less subtle coercion, just as workers in an economic system act in response to incentives and constraints.

Rubin and her allies would no doubt be appalled by any association between themselves and the British prime minister Margaret Thatcher, but their approach to sexual ethics is nicely summed up by Thatcher's declaration, during a 1987 interview, that 'there's no such thing as society.' The phrase has since become notorious in British politics, often interpreted by Thatcher's critics as expressive of a greedy and often brutal individualism that she is taken to represent. Despite her party allegiance, Thatcher was not a conservative with a small 'c' because she did not seek to conserve. She deliberately pursued a process of creative destruction, stripping out the old to make way for the new. Her supporters insist that this was a necessity – that the coal mining industry, for instance, had no more life left in it – but her critics point out that the disruption brought about by her aggressive interventions has led to long-term misery, particularly in areas of Britain that are now post-industrial, and that this misery ultimately led to the further disruption heralded by the Brexit referendum of 2016.

Thatcher did not obey G. K. Chesterton's directive, laid out in this famous passage:

> In the matter of reforming things, as distinct from deforming them, there is one plain and simple principle; a principle which will probably be called a paradox. There exists in such a case a certain institution or law; let us say, for the sake of simplicity, a fence or gate erected across a road. The more modern type of reformer goes gaily up to it and says, 'I don't see the use of this; let us clear it away.' To which the more intelligent type of reformer will do well to answer: 'If you don't see the use of it, I certainly won't let you clear it away. Go away and think. Then, when you can come back and tell me that you do see the use of it, I may allow you to destroy it.'[9]

Chesterton points out that the person who doesn't understand the purpose of a social institution is *the last person* who should be allowed to reform it. The world is big and dynamic – so much so that literally no one is capable of fully understanding it or predicting how its systems might respond to change. The parable of 'Chesterton's Fence' ought to encourage caution in would-be reformers, because there *is* such a thing as society, and it is more complex than any of us can fathom.

But the sexual Thatcherites do not recognise the delicate and relational nature of a sexual culture and therefore cannot see that society is composed of both pikes and minnows, as well as people who may play both roles at different times ('half victim, half accomplice', as Simone de Beauvoir put it). Their analysis can only understand people as freewheeling, atomised individuals, all out looking out for number one and all up for a good time. Thus when they see a taboo – against, say, having sex with chicken corpses – they assume that, if no obvious purpose for the taboo springs to mind, it must therefore be unnecessary. They falsely assume that, with all such taboos removed, then we would all be liberated and capable of making entirely free choices about our sexual lives, sampling from a menu of delightful options made newly available by the sexual revolution ('What will sir have today – the chicken?').

But in fact our choices are severely constrained, not only because we are impressionable creatures who absorb the values and ideas of our surrounding culture but also because sex is a social activity: it requires the involvement of other people. If I am, for instance, a young female student looking for a boyfriend at my twenty-first-century university, and I don't want to have sex before marriage, then I will find my options limited in a way that they wouldn't have been seventy years ago. When sex before marriage is expected, and when almost all of the other women participating in my particular sexual market are willing to 'put out' on a first or second date, then *not* being willing to do the same becomes a competitive disadvantage. The abstinent young woman must either be tremendously attractive, in order to out-compete her more permissive peers, or she must be happy to restrict her dating pool only to those men who are as unusual as she is. Being eccentric carries costs.

The 'progress' narrative disguises the challenge of interconnectedness by presenting history as a simple upward trajectory, with all of us becoming steadily more free as old-fashioned restrictions are surmounted. But there is another way of understanding history – a way that is perhaps less reassuring but which is able to incorporate the inevitable fact of conflict and trade-offs.

The wrong side of history

We should reject the progress narrative, looking instead to those such as the Marxist critic Raymond Williams who remind us that societies are always in a state of flux. At any one time, Williams writes, there will be dominant, residual and emergent cultural elements existing simultaneously and in tension with one another.[10] We tend to celebrate those historical figures who were part of emergent strains that later became dominant: the people credited with being ahead of their time and later vindicated, sometimes only (and most romantically) in death. But we usually pay less attention to the people who found themselves part of residual elements that may once have been dominant but eventually faded away. We venerate the people whose ideologies won out, perhaps imagining ourselves to be among their number. We think a lot less about the people who lost.

The infamous campaigner Mary Whitehouse is one of history's losers. Born in 1910, she never let go of her Edwardian sensibilities, even as the society she knew collapsed around her ears. She spent thirty-seven years organising letter-writing campaigns in an effort to halt the arrival of what she called the 'permissive society', horrified as she was by the displays of sex and violence that suddenly appeared on British television screens from the 1960s onwards. A contemporary of Whitehouse's described her in the *Financial Times* as a 'little Canute, exhorting the waves of moral turpitude to retreat'.[11] She didn't campaign for change, she campaigned for stasis. And she failed utterly, in a grand display of public humiliation.

Some of Whitehouse's concerns look rather silly now. She and her fellow campaigners expended a huge amount of energy on the kind of sauciness that nowadays seems quaint. The double entendres in songs such as Chuck Berry's 'My Ding-a-Ling' and sitcoms such as *It Ain't Half Hot Mum* all provoked letters, as did a suggestively placed microphone during Mick Jagger's appearance on *Top of the Pops*.

One of Whitehouse's first forays into public life was an anonymous 1953 piece for the *Sunday Times* that advised mothers on how best to inhibit homosexuality in their sons. This open homophobia was combined with a crusade against blasphemy that often called upon archaic legislation. In 1977, she pursued a private prosecution against *Gay News* for printing a poem that described a Roman centurion fantasising about having sex with the body of the crucified Christ. The editor was convicted of blasphemous libel, and the QC who represented him later wrote that Whitehouse's 'fear of homosexuals was visceral' – he may well have been right.[12]

Her reputation as a bigoted fuddy-duddy means that, if Whitehouse is remembered now, it is usually as a punchline. And indeed in her own lifetime she was the subject of constant ridicule. One of her books was ritually burned on a BBC sitcom, her name was used in jest as the title of the hit comedy show *The Mary Whitehouse Experience*, and a porn star mockingly changed her name to 'Mary Whitehouse' by deed poll (this second Mary Whitehouse later committed suicide). Sir Hugh Greene, director general of the BBC between 1960 and 1969, openly despised Whitehouse, so much so that he purchased a grotesque naked portrait of her to hang in his office. The story goes that Greene would vent his frustration by throwing darts at the portrait, squealing with delight if he managed to hit one of Whitehouse's six breasts.[13]

Arch-progressive Owen Jones, columnist at *The Guardian*, is among those who now use Whitehouse's name as short-hand for being on the 'wrong side of history' (a phrase Jones often employs).[14] Such a framing presents Whitehouse as villainy incarnate, set against the romantic heroes of Raymond Williams's emergent strain – in this case, Sir Hugh Greene and his permissive allies. But this historical narrative only works if one is deliberately selective. Whitehouse has found herself condemned by 'history' on the issues of homosexuality, blasphemy, and the phallic use of microphones on *Top of the Pops*. But on one issue she was remarkably prescient: Whitehouse was one of the few public figures of her day who gave a damn about child sexual abuse.

At the same time that Sir Hugh Greene was lobbing darts at Whitehouse's naked portrait, his organisation was enabling abuses perpetrated against women and children by many famous men, including – most notoriously – the TV presenter Jimmy Savile. It was only after Savile died, unpunished, in 2011 that the scale of his crimes became clear. It is now believed that, over the course of at least forty years, BBC staff turned a blind eye to the rape and sexual assault of up to 1,000 girls and boys by Savile in the corporation's changing rooms and studios.[15] He abused many more victims, young and old, male and female, in hospitals, schools, and anywhere else he could seek them out. Savile's celebrity status enabled his sexual aggression, allowing him access to vulnerable victims, particularly children, and discouraging investigation.

Savile made little effort to conceal what he got up to, and indeed would often joke about it. Answering the phone to journalists, he would apparently greet them, unprompted, with the phrase 'She told me she was over sixteen', invariably met with nervous laughter.[16] In his autobiography, published in 1974, Savile openly admitted to some of his crimes, for instance writing of a time, before he became a TV presenter, when he had been running nightclubs in the north of England and a police officer asked him to look out for a young girl who had run away from a home for juvenile offenders. Savile told the officer that, if the girl showed up at one of his clubs, he would be sure to hand her over to the authorities – 'but I'll keep her all night first as my reward.' The girl *did* show up at one of his clubs, and he *did* spend the night with her, but no criminal action was ever taken.[17] Savile told this story openly, as if it were funny, and seemingly without fear of consequences.

When the Savile scandal broke in the early 2010s, the same refrain was repeated by commentators again and again: 'It was a different time.'[18] And indeed it was, although we sometimes forget quite how different attitudes towards child sexual abuse really were during the 1970s and 1980s. In Britain, members of the Paedophile Information Exchange were openly campaigning for the abolition of the age of consent and found themselves welcomed warmly in some establishment circles, with Margaret Thatcher's government refusing demands to ban the group.[19] In the United States, NAMBLA (the 'North American Man Boy Love Association') was founded at the end of the 1970s and attracted support from figures including the poet Allen Ginsberg and the feminist Camille Paglia.[20]

In some European countries at this time, child pornography was freely available, having been legalised at the same time as other forms of pornography from the end of the 1960s.[21] In Sweden, for instance, it emerged in 2009 that the Royal Library in Stockholm was in possession of a collection of child pornography acquired (legally) between 1971 and 1980 and still being loaned (illegally) to members of the public into the twenty-first century[22] – an uncomfortable reminder of Sweden's hyper-liberal past.

In 1977, a petition to the French parliament calling for the decriminalisation of sex between adults and children was signed by a long list of famous intellectuals, including

Jean-Paul Sartre, Jacques Derrida, Louis Althusser, Roland Barthes, Simone de Beauvoir, Gilles Deleuze, Félix Guattari and – that esteemed radical and father of Queer Theory – Michel Foucault.[23] In 2021, the writer Guy Sorman alleged in an interview with *The Times* that Foucault had also acted on this political principle, sexually abusing children aged between about eight and ten during the period when he lived in Tunisia in the late 1960s. Sorman claimed that this fact was known to his fellow journalists, 'but nobody did stories like that in those days. Foucault was the philosopher king. He's like our god in France.'[24]

All of these figures now find themselves (as Owen Jones would term it) on 'the wrong side of history', since the 1990s saw a sharp swing back against efforts to normalise paedophilia. During the 1970s it was primarily 'regressive' conservatives who opposed groups such as the Paedophile Information Exchange, with Mary Whitehouse, for instance, lobbying hard for the private member's bill that became the Protection of Children Act 1978. Eventually, Whitehouse was joined by progressives in her condemnation of child sexual abuse, but her contribution was erased and the shameful history of the liberal tolerance for paedophilia in the decades following the sexual revolution was mostly forgotten, to be rediscovered, piecemeal, during investigations such as the one into Jimmy Savile.

Paedophilia is now condemned by liberals and conservatives alike, alongside a clutch of other paraphilias, including necrophilia and bestiality. For liberals, the wall between licit and illicit sexual behaviour is now built upon an emphasis on consent, which I'll explore in greater depth in the coming chapters. The problem with paedophilia, according to this argument, is that children can't consent, and therefore any sexual activity involving them will always be unacceptable. Thus, if the paedophilia apologism of sexual revolutionaries such as Foucault and Rubin is remembered at all, it is as a brief and embarrassing detour from the progressive path – a kink (so to speak) in the arc of the moral universe's bend towards justice.

But, upon closer scrutiny, the consent argument falls apart. Liberals may be able to accept the banning of child porn without any qualms, since it necessitates the abuse of real children in its production, but what about images that the police term 'pseudo-photographs' that appear to depict real children? What about illustrations? What about adults dressing up and pretending to be children during sex? What about porn performers who appear to be very young? What about porn performers who deliberately make themselves look even younger? What about Belle Delphine, the 21-year-old social media star, who sells pornographic images of herself wearing braces and girlish clothes and in 2021 was criticised for sharing images of herself seemingly dressed as a child and pretending to be raped by a man dressed as a kidnapper? Defending herself against her critics, Delphine insisted: 'I am not apologising for anything, what I did wasn't wrong, and much more normal than people think. Look at one of the most common sexual outfits and fantasies, schoolgirl. If you wear that are you promoting paedophilia now?'[25]

Within the liberal framework, how can we respond to Delphine's question with the answer that, for most of us, is intuitive: 'Yes, schoolgirl fantasies do promote paedophilia'? An ethical system based solely on consent does not allow space for this kind of moral intuition, which puts liberals into an awkward position, as Jonathan Haidt's research has shown. It is difficult to invoke J. S. Mill's harm principle when faced with a wide range of alarming sexual scenarios: consensual incest, cannibalism, sex with dead chickens, and sex acts that are at the very least paedophilic-adjacent, if not outright paedophilic.

Breaking taboos

When you set out to break down sexual taboos, you shouldn't be surprised when *all* taboos are considered fair game for breaking, including the ones you'd rather retain. The claim from Foucault and his allies was never that violently coercing children into sex is OK. Rather, they claimed that sexual desire develops earlier in some children than in others and that it is therefore possible in some cases for children to have sexual relationships with adults that are not only *not* traumatic but mutually enjoyable. The claim, therefore, was not that consent is unimportant but, rather, that children are sometimes capable of consenting. And they pointed out, correctly, that paedophiles are a maligned sexual minority who suffer greatly as a result of the taboo maintained against them. Their project, therefore, was not a detour from the progressive path but in fact logically in keeping with it. The principles of sexual liberalism do, I'm sorry to say, trundle inexorably towards this endpoint, whether or not we want them to.

And, indeed, after the intense backlash against paedophilia advocacy in the 1990s and early 2000s, we are now starting to see some slippage back towards the thinking of the 1970s. In 2020, Netflix released a film called *Cuties* (originally *Mignonnes*), written and directed by the French-Senegalese filmmaker Maïmouna Doucouré. The protagonist is eleven-year-old Amy, who lives with her Senegalese family in a poor district of Paris. When Amy's father announces his intention to take a second wife, Amy and her mother are heartbroken, and the rupture pushes Amy away from her conservative religious community and into the orbit of a group of girls who call themselves the Cuties.

The Cuties are not nice girls. They bully Amy and each other, they physically attack other children, they steal, they lie, and they also twerk. Aged eleven, they have formed an amateur dance troupe and adopted skimpy outfits and a gyrating style that is a world away from anything Amy has experienced before. The girls aren't directly groomed by anyone, and in fact we never see any overt acts of sexual aggression. They learn to grind and pout via the internet, particularly a social media marketplace in which pre-teen sexualisation is well rewarded with likes and follows. In one scene, Amy sits among older women in prayer, while under her veil she furtively watches video on her stolen smartphone of adult women slapping each other's naked buttocks. Thrilled by the aesthetic, Amy teaches the other girls to add more explicit moves to their routine, and in one particularly unwatchable scene the children encourage each other to jiggle their tiny backsides and hump the floor in an imitation of pornified ecstasy.

This scene goes on forever, as do half a dozen other similar scenes, one of which was widely shared online when the film became a crucial wedge issue in an international culture war – so much so that #CancelNetflix trended on Twitter on and off for weeks, and some American Republicans demanded that Netflix executives face a criminal investigation for, as Representative Jim Banks put it, 'distribution of child pornography'.[26] Both Netflix and Doucouré defended the film by pointing out that it was intended as a commentary on the harms of child sexualisation. The problem was that it also featured a lot of *actual* child sexualisation, and the original marketing for the film played on this theme, with the four very young actresses dressed in glorified bikinis and arranged in suggestive poses. Gritty depictions of child sexualisation are not entirely new. *Taxi Driver* (1976), *Pretty Babies* (1978) and *Thirteen* (2003) all portrayed pre-pubescent girls in sexually inappropriate scenarios. But *Cuties* went further than any of these films in not only suggesting sexualisation but actually showing it, and at length.

Nevertheless, *Cuties* received positive reviews in outlets including the *Washington Post*, *Rolling Stone*, the *New Yorker* and *The Telegraph*,[27] whose critic praised this act of provocation in 'an age terrified of child sexuality' and later tweeted his delight that the film had 'pissed off all the right people'. The word 'hysterical' recurred in these reviews, alongside the suggestion that the outrage over *Cuties* was wholly disproportionate, derived solely from a conservative moral panic over paedophilia.

There is something about paedophilia anxiety that is currently considered rather low status among the liberal elites. It is associated, particularly in America, with sinister groups such as QAnon and, particularly in Britain, with the tabloid newspapers. In 2000, Yvette Cloete, a thirty-year-old South African working as a trainee paediatrician in the Welsh county of Gwent, came home to find the word 'Paedo' painted on her front door. Police believed this to have been the work of local teenagers. Cloete gave a couple of interviews to the press in which she suggested that the vandals might have confused the word 'paediatrician' with 'paedophile', and the story took off, eventually becoming an urban legend. Among my peers, I have several times heard a version in which a local mob, whipped up by an anti-paedophilia campaign in the *News of the World*, physically attacks the paediatrician and even burns her house to the ground. As the journalist Brendan O'Neill wrote in 2010, the incident 'has been transformed by opinion-formers into proof that some communities are so dumb, morally bereft and easily swayed by paedophile-baiting tabloids like the News of the World that they end up confusing a good woman who helps children with evil men who rape them.'[28]

The story was popularised and distorted because it scratched a certain itch for snobbish progressives, presenting anti-paedophilia anxiety as an obsession of the ignorant and credulous working classes, a group very much considered to be on 'the wrong side of history'. But, while it is certainly true that the conspiracy theories generated by groups such as QAnon are false, it is also true that there have been some shocking examples of child sexual abuse taking place at scale and without detection. Jimmy Savile abusing up to a thousand children on BBC premises would sound like a conspiracy theory if we didn't know it to be true, just as Jeffrey Epstein supplying underage girls to famous and powerful men sounds like particularly bizarre fiction. And yet these things really happened.

The virtue of repression

In an episode of *The Simpsons* called 'I Am Furious (Yellow)', first aired in 2002, Homer Simpson decides to become a less angry person. Every time Homer finds himself feeling angry, he represses the emotion, and a lump appears on his neck. Soon enough, Homer's neck is covered in lumps and his calm demeanour is becoming increasingly fragile. At the end of the episode, Bart and Milhouse play a prank on Homer, and all of this repressed anger is suddenly released in an uncontrolled rampage. Later in hospital, the doctor informs the Simpson family that Homer's attempts at emotional repression could have proved lethal since, without the opportunity for release, 'the anger would've overwhelmed his nervous system.' Repression, it seems, is not only difficult but also dangerous.

This is a comical representation of a particular understanding of Freud that is popular in the contemporary West and which is applied to sexual repression just as much as to emotional repression. This model understands sexual desire to be a fixed quantity which must be periodically released, either through actual intercourse or through some other kind of 'safety valve', such as porn.

The problem with this model is that it does not recognise the necessity of sexual repression. Even in a post-1960s sexual free market, the law often requires us to repress our sexual impulses. If you want to have sex with someone, but they either won't or can't consent, then the law obliges you to repress your desire. You are also forbidden from having sex with an animal or having sex with a corpse, and, in England and Wales, as well as in most other jurisdictions, you can't legally watch porn that features bestiality or necrophilia. What's more, you may risk imprisonment if you masturbate or have sex in a public place, a fact that outrages the Queer Theorist Pat Califia, who asks:

> Why is sex supposed to be invisible? Other pleasurable acts or acts of communication are routinely performed in public – eating, drinking, talking, watching movies, writing letters, studying or teaching, telling jokes and laughing, appreciating fine art. Is sex so deadly, hateful, and horrific that we can't permit it to be seen? Are naked bodies so ugly or so shameful that we can't survive the sight of bare tushes or genitals without withering away?[29]

Unfortunately for Califia, public opinion has not aligned with this particular act of taboo-breaking. Every society requires that some kinds of sexual impulse be repressed – what varies is where exactly the line is drawn.

The word 'Victorian' is often used in association with sexual repression, most likely because, in the historical pendulum swing back and forth on the issue of licentiousness, Victorian Britain is our most recent example of an intense swing towards the prudish. Although, as revisionist historians such as Matthew Sweet have pointed out, the popular characterisation of the Victorians as scandalised by unclothed table legs is not quite true,[30] and this was in fact a society riven with contradictions – for instance combining a sometimes sickeningly sentimental attitude towards children with widespread child prostitution and, until 1875, an age of consent set at just twelve.

But there is no doubt that the Victorians did indeed set the repressive bar higher than we now do, and that this resulted in terrible cruelties, primarily against gay men and unmarried mothers. Sexual repression is a blunt instrument, but it is not one we can do away with altogether, as the errors of the 1970s show. The radical desires of sexual liberals do not work in a world in which human sexuality is not always beautiful but often wicked and repulsive. The desire to free the minnows is a good one, but reckless action can result in freedom for the pikes as well. In an interconnected society, the one impacts the other.

But the progressive narrative disguises this truth and, in doing so, does terrible harm to the minnows: that is, the people who have been offered up as sacrifices to the cause of sexual freedom. A society that prioritises the desires of the highly sociosexual is necessarily one that prioritises the desires of men, given the natural distribution of this trait, and those men then need to call on other people – mostly young women – to satisfy their desires.

The sexual Thatcherites will dismiss this problem by insisting that the minnows are perfectly capable of exercising their own freedom by saying 'no'. They might even suggest that I am being patronising in describing anyone as a 'minnow' in the first place. But I imagine that many readers will be able to recall instances when this attempt at exercising agency in the face of sexual coercion has not worked for them, or for someone else, in the same way that most of us can recall instances when someone we know has been taken advantage of by an employer in some way. The sexual playing field is not even, but it suits the interests of the powerful to pretend that it is.

When we strip back all sexual morality to the bare bones, leaving only the principle of consent, we leave the way clear for some particularly predatory pikes. As the example of paedophilia advocacy shows, the consent framework is nowhere near robust enough to protect the vulnerable from harm. Given the profound importance and complexity of sexual relationships, a much more sophisticated moral system is required, and the Foucaults and Rubins of the world are not best placed to describe it.

Reverting to traditionalism doesn't solve the problem. Although I reject the chronological snobbery of progressivism that dismisses the dead as stupid and malevolent, the world we live in now is very far removed from the world in which the ancient religious codes were formulated. Our ancestors were confronted with material conditions that are wildly different from our own: they had no reliable contraception, lived in smaller and less complex societies, experienced very high birth and death rates, and by necessity assigned starkly different social and economic roles to men and women. Imitating the past cannot teach us how to live in the twenty-first century.

Appealing to moral intuition takes us some of the way. Sexual liberalism asks us to train ourselves out of the kind of instinctive revulsion that often has a protective function. I opened this chapter with some extreme examples of sexual behaviour that may be disturbing but are difficult to condemn within the liberal framework. There are plenty of real-life examples that are hardly less extreme. For instance, in 2021, the American actor Armie Hammer made headlines when several of his exes came forward to accuse him of coercive behaviour. One former girlfriend, Courtney Vucekovich, described Hammer as 'obsessive' and reported that he 'did some things with me that I wasn't comfortable with.'[31] Another, Paige Lorenze, spoke about Hammer's 'controlling' behaviour, which gave her a 'kind of feeling sick to my stomach'.[32]

The odd thing about this particular #MeToo case is that it really shouldn't have come as a surprise to anyone. Hammer had a long history of openly admitting to having violent and degrading sexual tastes – not only did he tell *Playboy* back in 2013 that he liked choking women,[33] he also confessed to his girlfriends that he had a thing for cannibalism. Several of these women have since told journalists that Hammer enjoyed

inflicting pain on them during sex and that he also spoke about
his desire to break their bones, eat their skin and barbecue
their flesh.

You'd think this might have been a red flag. And yet the
women who had sexual relationships with Hammer seem to
have imbibed the sexually liberal belief that there is a bright line
between how a person behaves in the bedroom and how they
behave outside of it. So while they didn't exactly *like* Hammer's
interest in cannibalism, they didn't feel able to object to it
either. They suppressed their moral intuition and, in doing so,
were pulled into the orbit of a dangerous and abusive man. As
we'll see in chapter 6, this is a predictable consequence of the
liberal attitude towards BDSM, which is particularly ruinous to
naive, agreeable minnows.

Sexual liberalism is misguided in not only disregarding but
actively resisting moral intuition. And yet at the same time,
much like the principle of consent, intuition is too simplistic
to be serviceable on its own. We may be able to broadly agree
on the most outrageous examples (cannibalism, say), but one
person's gut instinct won't always be the same as another person's. Sibling or parental incest – supposedly a universal taboo,
according to many anthropologists – has become a popular
category on mainstream porn platforms, which suggests that
a not insubstantial minority of users have some interest in it.
Moral intuition can be a starting point, but it can also sometimes be a poor guide.

I can't pretend that this is an easy issue to resolve, because
'How should we behave sexually?' is really just another way of
asking 'How should we behave?' and, after millennia of effort,
we are nowhere near reaching an agreement on the answer
to that question. Nevertheless, here is my attempt at a contribution: we should treat our sexual partners with dignity.
We should not regard other people as merely body parts to
be enjoyed. We should aspire to love and mutuality in all of
our sexual relationships, regardless of whether they are gay or

straight. We should prioritise virtue over desire. We should not assume that any given feeling we discover in our hearts (or our loins) ought to be acted upon.

Armie Hammer should have repressed his desire to hurt his sexual partners and Jimmy Savile should have repressed his desire to sexually violate children. Doing so would have done them no harm, because some degree of sexual repression is good and necessary. The world would be a better place if such men were more ashamed of their desires and acted on that shame by mastering themselves. But it's not only the most appalling abusers who could do with putting virtue before desire. All of us are likely to be tempted by our worst instincts every now and again, and we are much more likely to indulge them in a culture that encourages hedonism.

Aziz Ansari, like Armie Hammer, is a celebrity who found himself caught up in a Me Too scandal – but, unlike Hammer, his misbehaviour was more ambiguous. On the night of 25 September 2017, Ansari went on a date with a woman publicly known only as 'Grace'. They went back to his house and then had some sexual contact that left Grace feeling deeply uncomfortable. Although she gently pulled away, mumbling her reluctance, Ansari tried again and again to initiate sex. Eventually, at his request, she gave him a blow job. He never used any force, and she never actually said 'no', but Grace was left feeling used. The next day, she texted Ansari telling him as much and he apologised for having 'misread things'. Several months later, she published her account on the website *babe*.[34]

Ansari's behaviour did not meet the legal threshold for rape because Grace did technically consent to their encounter. Ansari clearly assumed that Grace would want to have sex with him – both because of his celebrity status and because having sex after a first date is now normative among young, 'sexually liberated' Westerners. And Grace was therefore put in a position in which she had to make the case *against* their having sex, and she found it almost impossible to do so. Much

like the student I quoted in chapter 1, she instinctively wanted
to defend her sexual boundaries, but she was thwarted by a
culture in which 'it's just sex' is the dominant view. They were
two consenting adults who had just been on a date, and sex was
the expected way to end the night, so how could she say 'no'?

Following the publication of Grace's account, liberal
feminist commentators tried to condemn Ansari within
the consent framework, suggesting that, against the available evidence, their encounter hadn't been truly consensual.
Given that the need for consent is the only moral principle
left standing under the reign of sexual disenchantment, this
was the principle that had to be put to work. The problem is
that the presence of consent is such a very, very low bar – an
absolute bare minimum requirement, not an ideal. Ansari had
managed to jump this bar, but he had also failed to behave
well. In another era, his behaviour might have been described
as immoral or ungentlemanly, but these are not words that
liberal feminists feel comfortable using, given the icky asso-
ciations with religious conservatism. The only vocabulary
left available to them is that relating to consent, because the
ideological toolbox put together by liberal feminism contains
just one blunt implement, which – unsurprisingly – isn't up
to the job.

A sophisticated system of sexual ethics needs to demand
more of people, and, as the stronger and hornier sex, men must
demonstrate even greater restraint than women when faced
with temptation. The word 'chivalry' is now deeply unfashion-
able, but it describes something of what I'm calling for. As the
feminist theorist Mary Harrington writes:

> 'Chivalrous' social codes that encourage male protectiveness
> toward women are routinely read from an egalitarian perspec-
> tive as condescending and sexist. But . . . the cross-culturally
> well-documented greater male physical strength and propen-
> sity for violence makes such codes of chivalry overwhelmingly

advantageous to women, and their abolition in the name of feminism deeply unwise.[35]

In the coming chapters, I'll explore some of the self-interested reasons why men might choose, as R. H. Tawney phrased it almost a century ago, 'the deliberate acceptance of social restraints upon individual expansion'. But the motivation to demonstrate sexual virtue ought to go beyond self-interest. It isn't against the law to cheat on a partner, or to accept sexual favours from a person you don't respect, or very subtly to coerce someone into sex – as Aziz Ansari did with Grace – but it isn't decent either. There are a lot of sexual behaviours that are neither criminal nor good and about which the consent framework has very little to say. Somewhere in the uneasy space between sexual liberalism and traditionalism, it has to be possible to navigate a virtuous path.

4

Loveless Sex Is Not Empowering

In the first ever episode of *Sex and the City*, aired in 1998, the Manhattanite columnist, socialite and everywoman Carrie Bradshaw resolves to stop looking for 'Mr Perfect' and start enjoying herself. In that effort, she hooks up with an ex-boyfriend, 'a self-centred, withholding creep' to whom she no longer has any emotional attachment. She drops round at his place mid-afternoon, enjoys his offer of oral sex, and then leaves before he's had a chance to orgasm himself. Ignoring her disgruntled ex, Carrie tells us of her delight: 'As I began to get dressed, I realised that I'd done it. I'd just had sex like a man. I left feeling powerful, potent and incredibly alive. I felt like I owned this city. Nothing and no one could get in my way.'

In the hit TV show *The Fall*, aired in the mid-2010s, the gorgeous police superintendent Stella Gibson also relishes the chance to have sex 'like a man'. Recently arrived in a new city where she has been tasked with investigating a series of murders, she spots a hunky sergeant – her junior both in rank and in age – and invites him back to her hotel for sex. Discovering later that the man is married, Gibson is ostentatiously unconcerned, justifying her sexual adventurousness with a quote from the feminist Catharine MacKinnon: 'Man fucks woman;

subject verb object.' The implication is clear: this woman *fucks back*.

These examples tell us something important about how sexual liberation is conceptualised for women, with *Sex and the City* leading the charge going into the twenty-first century and *The Fall* now representing a new normal, with Stella Gibson ubiquitously described in the press as a 'strong female lead' ('She's so comfortable with herself', added actress Gillian Anderson, discussing her character in an interview for *The Sun*).[1]

Both of these protagonists demonstrate their sexual agency by having loveless, brusque sex with men they don't like. They show no regard for their partners' intimate lives and discard them immediately afterwards. The purpose of the encounter is both physical gratification and – explicitly in Bradshaw's case, implicitly in Gibson's – psychological gratification. They treat their partners as means, not ends, out of a desire for short-term pleasure. Thus it seems that what the phrase having sex 'like a man' really means, at least in these popular representations, is having sex *like an arsehole*.

Nevertheless, liberal feminism understands having sex 'like a man' as an obvious route by which women can free themselves from old-fashioned patriarchal expectations of chastity and obedience. If you believe that there is nothing wrong, per se, with instrumentalising other people in pursuit of your own sexual gratification, then this makes sense. And if you believe that men and women are both physically and psychologically much the same, save for a few hang-ups absorbed from a sex-negative culture, then why wouldn't you want women to have access to the kind of sexual fun that men have always enjoyed (the high-status ones, at least)? The position is purely reactive: since women have historically been punished for this kind of sexual behaviour, liberation must surely mean not only an end to such punishment but also an endorsement of what was once forbidden: fucking back.

The sex writer and TV producer Karley Sciortino is a particularly enthusiastic proponent of this view. To her mind, the sexual double standard – by which male promiscuity is viewed as neutral or positive while female promiscuity is frowned upon – is the product of socialisation within a culture that Sciortino considers to be oppressively anti-sex. The solution, as she sees it, is to train ourselves out of negative responses to what she would call 'sluttiness':

> Today we've created an environment where (allegedly predatory) male sexuality needs to be policed, and (allegedly passive) female sexuality needs to be protected ... It's outdated, it's offensive, and it's psychologically destructive for women, because it has the power to mislead girls into thinking that having one not-ideal sexual experience means that they have lost part of themselves. *Hello* – pitying and victimising women doesn't help us: it just dismisses the importance of female sexual agency.[2]

The ambiguous term 'not-ideal' is doing a lot of work here, because Sciortino does acknowledge that the playing field is not entirely even, with or without the continued existence of slut shaming. For one thing, there is the difference in physical strength that means that any heterosexual encounter will inevitably be more dangerous for the woman. For another, there is the risk of pregnancy.

But the liberal feminist argument leads us to conclude that, if you are going to destroy the sexual double standard, then you must use your own body, and the bodies of other women, as a battering ram against the patriarchal edifice. The advice to young women is that you *must* 'fuck back' if you want to be a good feminist, and mostly it will turn out OK – and when it doesn't? When a sexual encounter turns out to be 'not-ideal', or worse? Well then, we must fall back on liberal feminism's old standby: 'teach men not to rape.'

The problem with this position is that 'fake it till you make it' is not a viable political strategy. We cannot just pretend that the world is safe and that the existence of 'predatory male sexuality' is no more than an outdated stereotype. As we saw in chapter 2, the global picture of sexual violence actually conforms very closely to stereotype — it really is men who perpetrate it, and it really is young women who are most at risk. This isn't a reality we can just wish away.

The sociosexuality gap

Men and women are not the same, either physically or psychologically. Casual heterosexual sex inherently carries much greater risks for women, and in return for much meaner rewards. And yet the (perfectly reasonable) insistence that women should be *allowed* to 'fuck back' without suffering criminalisation or social ostracisation slips all too easily towards the insistence that they therefore *ought to*. Carrie Bradshaw and Stella Gibson are, crucially, aspirational characters: attractive, glamorous and professionally successful. Their model is one that we are supposed to follow, and Sciortino encourages her readers to do so. I don't doubt that there are some women who genuinely enjoy casual sex and who decide, having weighed the risks and benefits, that it is in their best interests to pursue it. What I question is the claim that *a culture of casual sex* is somehow of benefit to women as a group.

I've written earlier in this book about what psychologists term 'sociosexuality' – the trait that determines a person's interest in sexual variety and adventure. The standard questionnaire used by researchers to assess sociosexuality asks respondents the following questions:[3]

- With how many different partners have you had sex within the past 12 months?

- With how many different partners have you had sexual intercourse on one and only one occasion?
- With how many different partners have you had sexual intercourse without having an interest in a long-term committed relationship with this person?
- Do you agree that sex without love is OK?
- Can you imagine being comfortable and enjoying 'casual' sex with different partners?
- Do you only want to have sex with a person when you are sure that you will have a long-term, serious relationship?
- How often do you have fantasies about having sex with someone you are not in a committed romantic relationship with?
- How often do you experience sexual arousal when you are in contact with someone you are not in a committed romantic relationship with?
- In everyday life, how often do you have spontaneous fantasies about having sex with someone you have just met?

Worldwide, there is a significant difference in average sociosexuality between the sexes, with men generally much keener to sow their wild oats than women are. And there is a compelling evolutionary explanation for this difference.[4] As the biologist Anne Campbell writes:

Biologically speaking, men's investment is completed at conception and they are free to move on to pastures new. But women, unlike men, are quality not quantity specialists. Their investment is not limited to a few moments' pleasure – they are committed to the reproductive consequences and women produce only a limited number of offspring . . . So great is the commitment demanded by every child that women's bodies and minds are exquisitely crafted to invest only in the highest-quality child that they can produce.[5]

Although it's typical for men to invest a great deal of time and energy into offspring produced within a socially recognised relationship (in other words, a marriage), men also have an alternative mode of sexuality in which they favour quantity of offspring over quality – that is, inseminating as many women as possible and not hanging around to deal with the consequences. This alternative mode is favoured more by some individual men than others, depending on their degree of sociosexuality – 'cads' versus 'dads' – but the difference is not absolute. Some men may be drawn more towards one sexual strategy than the other at certain points in their lives, or in certain situations, or with certain partners. There is a remarkable flexibility within male sexuality that women are not always aware of, particularly within a political environment that denies the existence of evolved psychological differences between the sexes.

It is crucial to remember that the sociosexuality difference between the sexes is an average one: there are some women who are exceptionally high in sociosexuality and there are some men who are low in it. This means that, at the individual level, if you know a person's sex, you cannot know for certain whether or not they will be highly sociosexual, although you can make an educated guess.

At the same time, it is also crucial to remember that individual exceptions to the rule do not negate the rule. For instance, the average differences in male and female sexuality become glaringly obvious when we look at the gay and lesbian communities. Although it may be controversial to point out how dramatically these two sexual cultures differ, there is plenty of hard data that it would be dishonest to ignore. Lesbian women are remarkably keen on committed monogamy: the median lesbian woman in the UK reports just one sexual partner within the last year,[6] and a majority report having known their sexual partners for months or years before they first had sex.[7] Lesbian women are also significantly more likely than gay men to get married or enter into a civil partnership.[8] In his memoir about gay life in America in the twentieth and twenty-first centuries, Andrew Sullivan writes of the lesbian community that 'here is a culture of extraordinary stability and variety, a monogamist's dream' – although, as he quite rightly notes, this is nevertheless a community 'which somehow has not found its champions among the family-mongering religious right.'[9]

In contrast, Sullivan describes the 'landscape of gay life' as 'almost a painting in testosterone',[10] and surveys on gay men's sexual behaviour confirm this characterisation, with casual sex very much more common in the gay community than in the lesbian community. Although, having said this, the *flexibility* of male sexuality is even more striking among gay men than it is among the straight. In one representative survey from 2010, roughly a quarter of gay men report being just as stably monogamous as the average lesbian, while another quarter report more than thirteen male partners within the last year,[11] and a smaller (but not insignificant) minority report hundreds of sexual partners across their lifetimes, which is almost unheard of among lesbian women – there is, after all, no lesbian equivalent of bathhouse culture. As the authors of the Gay Men's Sexual Survey put it: 'There is a very wide range of sexual partner change among men who have sex with men – many men have only one partner, many men have a different partner each week (or more often).'[12]

The minority of gay men who are highly sociosexual have a significant effect on the data – one large survey from 2016, for instance, found that the mean number of lifetime sexual partners is six times and eight times higher among gay and bisexual men, respectively, compared with straight men.[13] Thus sexual behaviour among gay men is an exceptionally good indicator of what happens when the limiting factor of female sexual preference is entirely removed.

Straight men's sexual preferences are constrained by the fact that, when women are given a choice, they are generally much pickier than men and reject a much larger proportion of suitors. For instance, one study from 1978 – since repeated, with exactly the same findings – involved participants of average attractiveness approaching strangers of a similar age and propositioning them for sex.[14] As the authors write: 'The great majority of men were willing to have a sexual liaison with the women who approach them. Not one woman agreed to a sexual liaison.'

Some feminists would attribute this to a sex-negative culture in which women suffer greater reputational damage when they are seen as being too promiscuous, and it may also be the case that some of the women involved in these studies might have wanted to accept the proposition but refused out of fear for their physical safety. However, these explanations cannot account for the fact that women are also much pickier on dating apps and websites than men are, and that men and women differ dramatically in their baseline levels of sexual disgust.[15] Disgust induces a physiological response that can be measured through heart and respiration rate, blood pressure and salivation, although the individual may not be aware of these indicators,[16] and studies find that, on average, the sexual disgust threshold is much lower for women than it is for men.

Curiously, I am not aware of any word in the English language for a particular emotion that every woman to whom I've spoken has experienced at least once, but that the men to whom I've spoken don't seem to recognise at all. It is a combination of both sexual disgust and fear – the bone-deep, nauseating feeling of being trapped in proximity to a horny man who repulses you. Being groped in a crowd, or leered at while travelling alone, or propositioned a little too forcefully in a bar – all of these situations can provoke this horrible emotion. It is an emotion that women in the sex industry are forced to repress. In fact, as the prostitution survivor Rachel Moran has written, the ability not to cry or vomit in response to sexual fear and disgust is one of the essential 'skills' demanded by the industry.[17]

More than any other area of life, prostitution reveals the sometimes vast differences between male and female sexual behaviour. Women make up the overwhelming majority of sex sellers, for the simple reason that almost all sex buyers are male (at least 99 per cent in every part of the world), most men are straight, and the industry is driven by demand. The absence of female sex buyers may partly be a consequence of the physical risks involved in a sexual encounter with a stranger, but this sex skew is also about the nature of male and female desire.

Sex buyers, by definition, are people who seek out sex outside of a committed relationship, usually with a person they have never met before, and this kind of sexual encounter is far, far more likely to appeal to people high in sociosexuality. People low in this trait *are just not interested* in having sex with a stranger, and are certainly not willing to pay money to do so or to risk punishment in countries where prostitution is fully or partially illegal. Male and female sociosexuality can be drawn (roughly) as two bell curves with a substantial overlap. But, as with any normally distributed trait, any average group difference will be most glaring at the tails. The people exceptionally high in sociosexuality are overwhelmingly men, and the people exceptionally low in it are overwhelmingly women. This means that, as a rule, any sexual culture that encourages women to 'fuck back' will, more often than not, just encourage women to fuck themselves over.

A hand held in daylight

The heterosexual dating market has a problem, and it's not one that can be easily resolved. Male sexuality and female sexuality, at the population level, do not match. On average, men want casual sex more often than women do, and women want committed monogamy more often than men do. Hook-up culture demands that women suppress their natural instincts in order to match male sexuality and thus meet the male demand for no-strings sex. Some women are quite happy to do this, but most women find it unpleasant, or even distressing. Thus hook-up culture is a solution to the sexuality mismatch that benefits some men at the expense of most women.

I propose a different solution, based on a fundamental feminist claim: unwanted sex is worse than sexual frustration. I'm not willing to accept a sexual culture that puts pressure on people low in sociosexuality (overwhelmingly women) to meet the sexual demands of those high in sociosexuality (overwhelmingly men), particularly when sex carries so many more risks for women, in terms of violence and pregnancy. Hook-up culture is a terrible deal for women and yet has been presented by liberal feminism as a form of liberation. A truly feminist project would demand that, in the straight dating world, it should be men, not women, who adjust their sexual appetites.

This argument is a long way from the feminist mainstream in the twenty-first century. Progressive media outlets churn out articles with such headlines as 'Your 7-point intersectional feminist guide to hook ups' and '5 fantastic ways to engage in feminist hookup culture', all arguing that, with consent, anything goes.[18] But this approach fails to recognise the relational nature of sex and the competitive nature of the sexual marketplace, overstating the extent to which any of us can make truly free choices in a system in which we are all radically restricted. And it leaves no space for the sociosexuality gap – after all, how could it? Liberal feminism can hardly bear to recognise the existence of *physical* differences between the sexes, let alone psychological ones.

In a darkly funny article published in 2020, *Elle* magazine wrestles with some of the problems thrown up by hook-up culture,[19] but it does so within an ideological framework that cannot accommodate the fact of sexual conflict. Rather than recognise the difference between men and women on this most crucial of issues, the writers instead attempt to carve out a new, gender-neutral sexual minority of 'demisexuals', a 'select few members of society', who just aren't enthused about casual sex:

> Struggling to identify with her sexuality for years, in 2016 Washington Post writer Meryl Williams detailed how she came across the term 'demisexuality' on Twitter and started an investigation into what it meant, which ultimately helped her come to terms with her own sexual orientation. 'I'm just glad that a term for my sexuality exists, even if it's one I'll probably have to explain to my future partners,' she wrote.

What Williams is actually describing here is typical female sexuality. She isn't special: she's a normal woman who has just enough emotional insight to recognise that hook-up culture isn't good for her but is lacking the political insight to recognise the existence of a bigger problem.

A more depressing pop-feminist genre comes at the socio-sexuality gap from a different angle, advising women to work on overcoming their perfectly normal and healthy preference for intimacy and commitment in sexual relationships. Guides with titles such as 'Here's what to do if you start "catching feelings"', 'How to bio-hack your brain to have sex without getting emotionally attached' and 'How to have casual sex without getting emotionally attached' advise readers to, for instance, avoid making eye contact with their partners during sex, in an effort to avoid 'making an intimate connection'.[20] Readers are also advised to take cocaine or methamphetamines before sex to dull the dopamine response, but to avoid alcohol, since for women (but, tellingly, not men) this seems to increase 'the likelihood they will bond prematurely'. All sorts of innovative methods of dissociation are advised, for example: 'Another way to prevent the intimate association between your fuck buddy and the heightened activity in your brain's reward center is to consciously focus your thoughts on another person during sex.' These guides are all carefully phrased to present the problem as gender-neutral, but research on male and female attitudes towards casual sex, combined with what we know about the sociosexuality gap, makes clear that what is really happening here is that it is overwhelmingly *women* who are being advised to emotionally cripple themselves in order to gratify *men*.

In the West, hook-up culture is normative among adolescents and young adults – both popular culture and survey data indicate that sexual behaviour outside of traditional committed romantic relationships has become increasingly typical and socially acceptable.[21] And, although it is possible for young women to opt out, research suggests that only a minority do so.[22] Absent some kind of religious commitment, this is now the 'normal' route presented to girls as they become sexually active. And young people tend to be *very anxious* about being 'normal'.

Leah Fessler has written thoughtfully about her time as a student at Middlebury College, an institution in which hookup culture reigned and where abstinence seemed to be the only way in which a female student could avoid participating.[23] Unwilling to commit to celibacy, Fessler convinced herself that emotionless sex was the feminist thing to do, and she did her best to ignore her unhappiness:

> After I began having sex with these guys, the power balance always tipped. A few hookups in, I'd begin to obsess, primarily about the ambiguity of it all. My friends and I would analyze incessantly: Does he like me? Do you like him? He hasn't texted in a day. Read this text. I'm so confused. He said he didn't want anything, but keeps asking to hang out . . . With time, inevitably, came attachment. And with attachment came shame, anxiety, and emptiness.

The worst thing for women at Middlebury were the 'pseudo-relationships':

the mutant children of meaningless sex and loving partner-
ships. Two students consistently hook up with one another
– and typically, only each other – for weeks, months, even
years. Yet per unspoken social code, neither party is permitted
emotional involvement, commitment, or vulnerability. To call
them exclusive would be 'clingy,' or even 'crazy.'

Fessler and her friends quietly admitted to each other that
what they really wanted was true intimacy: public recognition
of a relationship, an arm around the waist, 'a hand held in
daylight'. She wrote her senior year thesis on hook-up culture
at Middlebury, and, of the straight women who participated in
her research, 100 per cent of interviewees and three-quarters
of survey respondents stated a clear preference for committed
relationships. Only 8 per cent of women who said they were
presently in pseudo-relationships reported being 'happy' with
their situation. Other studies consistently find the same thing:
following hook-ups, women are more likely than men to experience regret, low self-esteem and mental distress.[24] And, most
of the time, they don't even orgasm.

Female pleasure is rare during casual sex. Men in casual
relationships are just not as good at bringing women to orgasm
in comparison with men in committed relationships – in first
time hook-ups, only 10 per cent of women orgasm, compared
to 68 per cent of women in long-term relationships.[25] This is
partly a consequence of the fact that men who are familiar with
their partner's bodies and sexual preferences are better placed
to know what they want, but another factor is the so-called
sexual script for casual encounters, which is more likely to
prioritise male desire.

We know that, since the turn of the century, rates of anal
sex and fellatio have been rising among young adults while
rates of cunnilingus have declined, likely a consequence of the
influence of internet porn.[26] These sex acts are much less likely
to result in female orgasm, with anal sex, in particular, usually

offering pain without pleasure for anyone lacking a prostate. One typical study has found that 30 per cent of women experience pain during vaginal sex, that 72 per cent experience pain during anal sex, and that 'large proportions' do not voice this discomfort to their partners.[27] These figures don't suggest a generation of women revelling in sexual liberation – instead, a lot of women seem to be having unpleasant, crappy sex out of a sense of obligation.

University campuses offer a particularly good venue for examining hook-up culture, with thousands of young people cooped up together, living and working in the same relatively closed environment. We can, for instance, learn a lot by looking at how the ratio between male and female students affects sexual cultures in these environments, and doing so reveals that the rise in the proportion of women in higher education since the second wave has had a perversely anti-woman effect on the sexual culture. As male students have become a scarcer resource, the balance of power seems to have tipped towards them, and, as one researcher writes: 'while women may run the clubs, dominate in classes, and generally define the character of the university, the law of supply and demand rules the social scene. That's why the women are both competitive in seeking men and submissive in lowering their standards.'[28]

Hook-up culture is more common in environments in which men are dominant, and, in a sexual marketplace in which such a culture prevails, a woman who refuses to participate puts herself at a disadvantage. As another group of researchers put it, 'some individual women may be capitulating to men's preferences for casual sexual encounters because, if they do not, someone else will.'[29]

And yet this is not, generally, how most women who participate in hook-up culture understand their behaviour – at least not at the time. Looked at coolly, we may be able to recognise the existence of a sexual marketplace with its own internal rules and incentive structure, and we can readily identify different interest groups within it. But that's usually not how real people *actually feel* about their sexual lives, which are not only intimate and messy but also bound up with complicated issues of self-esteem.

The liberal feminist narrative of sexual empowerment is popular for a reason: it is much more palatable to understand oneself as a sassy Carrie Bradshaw, making all the decisions and challenging the patriarchal status quo. Adopting such a self-image can be protective, making it easier to endure what is often, in fact, a rather miserable experience. If you're a young woman launched into a sexual culture that is fundamentally not geared towards protecting your safety or wellbeing, in which you are considered valuable in only a very narrow, physical sense, and if your only options seem to be either hooking up or strict celibacy, then a comforting myth of 'agency' can be attractive.

This myth depends on naiveté about the true nature of male sexuality. Today's young women are typically unaware that men are, in general, much better suited to emotionless sex and find it much easier to regard their sexual partners as disposable. Ignorant of this fact, women can all too easily fail to recognise that being desired is not at all the same thing as being held in high esteem. It isn't nice to think of oneself as disposable or to acknowledge that other people view you that way. Often, it's easier to turn away from any acknowledgement of what is really going on, at least temporarily. I've spoken to a lot of women who participated in hook-up culture when they were young and only years later came to realise just how unhappy it made them. I've yet to meet anyone who has travelled the same emotional journey, but in the opposite direction.

If you're a woman who's had casual sexual relationships with men in the past, you might try answering the following questions as honestly as you can:

1 Did you consider your virginity to be an embarrassing burden you wanted to be rid of?

2 Do you ever feel disgusted when you think about consensual sexual experiences you've had in the past?
3 Have you ever become emotionally attached to a casual sexual partner and concealed this attachment from him?
4 Have you ever done something sexually that you found painful or unpleasant and concealed this discomfort from your partner, either during sex or afterwards?

If your score is zero, then congratulations – your high sociosexuality and good luck have allowed you successfully to navigate a treacherous sexual marketplace. But if you answered 'yes' to any of these questions (as I suspect you probably did), you are entitled to feel angry at a sexual culture that set you up to fail.

Cads and dads

While most women assess both their short-term and their long-term partners based on the same criteria, most men do not.[30] A woman will typically look for identical qualities in a hook-up as she does in a husband: as the evolutionary biologist David Buss puts it, 'in both cases, women want someone who is kind, romantic, understanding, exciting, stable, healthy, humorous, and generous with his resources. In both contexts, women desire men who are tall, athletic, and attractive.'[31] Men, in contrast, tend to be very particular about the criteria they look for in a potential spouse but much less so when seeking out casual sex.

Sherry Argov, author of the best-selling dating advice book *Why Men Love Bitches*, puts it frankly: 'What men don't want women to know is that, almost immediately, they put women into one of two categories: "good time only" or "worthwhile." And the minute he slides you into that "good time only" category, you'll almost never come back out.'[32] There is a straightforward scientific reason for the existence of these two categories: it is hard to dissuade men out of their instinct to care about what evolutionary biologists call 'paternity certainty'. Men in 'cad' mode aren't concerned with the welfare of their unknown offspring, since they are favouring quantity over quality, but men in 'dad' mode care a great deal and will often devote their lives to providing for their families.

But 'dad' mode carries a significant cost in the form of jealousy. In our evolutionary history, men who unwittingly devoted themselves to raising children not genetically related to them were at a selection disadvantage, while those who practised what biologists call 'mate guarding' – i.e. behaving jealously – could be certain that their children were their own. The sexual double standard is the result of this mate-guarding instinct.

As with all other features of our evolutionary heritage, there is room for flexibility here. Plenty of men (and women) are utterly devoted to their adoptive or step-children, regardless of their genetic link. And a surprisingly high proportion of men privately express a sexual interest in cuckolding which may seem confusing within a strict evolutionary framework. However, in general the sexual double standard is so prevalent and so fiercely held that it is considered by some anthropologists to be a human universal.[33]

It was once much stronger in the West. Lawrence Stone writes in his history of divorce in England that until quite recently the double standard was formalised in law, with female adultery considered to be 'an unpardonable breach of the law of property and the idea of hereditary descent', whereas male adultery was 'regarded as a regrettable but understandable foible'.[34] And the British sociologist Anthony Giddens (born in 1938) describes the sexual culture that prevailed in the mid-twentieth century:

> Virginity on the part of girls prior to marriage was prized by both sexes. Few girls disclosed the fact if they allowed a boy-

friend to have full sexual intercourse – and many were only likely to permit such an act to happen once formally engaged to the boy in question. More sexually active girls were disparaged by the others, as well as by the very males who sought to 'take advantage' of them. Just as the social reputation of the girls rested upon their ability to resist, or contain, sexual advances, that of the boys rested upon the sexual conquests they could achieve.[35]

Although it may not be formalised in law or even explicitly spoken about in the post-sexual revolution era, the sexual double standard does persist. For adolescents, the association between lifetime number of sexual partners and peer status varies significantly by sex, such that greater numbers of sexual partners are positively correlated with boys' social status but negatively correlated with that of girls.[36] Among adults, promiscuity in men is generally viewed neutrally, whereas a woman's reputation among her peers is damaged as her number of sexual partners increases.[37] People may be reluctant actually to say so outright, but privately there is a social penalty suffered by women viewed as promiscuous.

When looking for a long-term partner, anonymous surveys suggest that the vast majority of straight men prefer to choose a wife with a limited sexual history and little interest in casual sex, past or present. Women also prefer a husband who is not unusually promiscuous, but their preference is not as strong, and most are willing to accept a man who has historically enjoyed casual sex but has since settled down.[38]

Importantly, however, men generally don't mind a more extensive sexual history when they're looking for a hook-up, or what Sherry Argov would call a 'good time only' partner. Then, in fact, promiscuity may increase the appeal. With a high sexual disgust threshold, a natural interest in sexual variety, no personal risk of pregnancy, and no fear of slut shaming, casual sex offers men a cornucopia of delights that are difficult to resist. And the liberal feminist narrative of 'fucking back' provides comfort for any man whose conscience might trouble him. With hook-up culture established as normative, both men and women are funnelled into patterns of behaviour that are grimly complementary. Men are encouraged into 'cad' mode, pursuing temporary relationships that offer all of the pleasures of cheap sex and none of the responsibilities of commitment. Meanwhile, women compete with each other for short-term male sexual attention, and may well win it, but in a form liable to induce (in Leah Fessler's words) 'shame, anxiety, and emptiness'.

Mutual incomprehension

Just like their female peers, men may not consciously realise that this is what they're participating in. And, in one sense, who can blame them? Teenage boys are raised on pop culture that presents having sex 'like a man' as the ultimate form of female sexual empowerment, and, in the porn to which they are typically exposed from childhood, women are shown *begging* men for painful or degrading sex acts. When young men start having sex offline, they will likely encounter women – themselves schooled by porn and pop culture – who hide their distress, fake their orgasms, work hard to avoid 'catching feelings', and in all other ways strive to be what Gillian Flynn has famously described as the 'Cool Girl', the woman who is 'above all hot': 'Hot and understanding. Cool Girls never get angry; they only smile in a chagrined, loving manner and let their men do whatever they want. Go ahead, shit on me, I don't mind, I'm the Cool Girl.'[39]

We should hardly be surprised when, after all this, many men assume that women *really don't mind* being relegated to 'good time only'. The resulting dysfunction can be glimpsed in posts such as this, on the r/relationships subreddit:

I was hanging out with my friends with benefits on Thursday after work. We been hooking up for six months. I was heating us up some food and she started asking about what I look in a long term girlfriend.

I told her that I want someone successful, and someone that I think would make a good mom. She starts then talking about how she has those qualities and I see how this conversation is going so I change the topic.

She brings it up and starts asking me what should she focus on to be the kind of girl guys want to marry one day. I told her she is fine the way she is, she just needs to find the right guy. She asked me why I don't want to date her down the road when I am looking for something.

I told her, that she is great, but she isn't really girlfriend material in my eyes. She started crying like crazy after that. I don't know what was going on we never had a thing, she never talked about having feelings or anything.[40]

Or this post, on a different subreddit:

I have been seeing my friends with benefits Kara for a while now, almost 8 months. We used to work together, now before you guys ask no she does not have a crush on me or emotionally likes me.

She has been single for a while and wants a guy similar to me if that makes sense, has a decent career etc, in decent shape.

Now honestly I think she is punching too high when it comes to a relationship. . . . I told her that she should focus less on physical traits like looks and be willing to look past them when dating guys. She asked me if I was telling her to lower her standards and I was like sort of. She got super offended.[41]

These men seem to be genuinely bewildered by the fact that the women they have been having sex with for many months are unhappy in these pseudo-relationships. And the women seem to have drifted into this arrangement, not realising how little regard their partners really have for them. This is a tragedy of mutual incomprehension.

However, I cannot help but harbour a sneaking suspicion that many men – perhaps all – do realise that operating in 'cad' mode is not actually harmless. Male readers who have ever had heterosexual casual sex might like to ask themselves these questions, a counterpart to the questions I addressed to female readers earlier in the chapter:

1 Have you ever had sex with a woman you'd be embarrassed to introduce to your friends?
2 Have you ever failed to contact a woman after sex?
3 Have you ever suspected that your casual partner was becoming emotionally attached to you and failed either to commit to or break off the relationship?
4 Have you ever encouraged a woman to do something sexually, even though she showed reluctance?

The answer to all of these questions ought to be 'no', but a culture of casual sex incentivises men to do such things, and generally with no social penalty. If anything, men who fuck and chuck 'good time only' women can often expect to increase their social status among their male peers, at least in the short term.

In a casual sex culture, the centre of gravity shifts towards the higher end of the sociosexuality spectrum, and this disproportionately benefits men. But that isn't to say that there isn't an eventual cost to be borne by the men who throw themselves into such a culture. A man's period of youthful desirability isn't as narrow as a woman's (which is really only twenty years, from late teens to late thirties), but the playboy period is still time limited – perhaps a third of a modern Western lifetime. A man in his twenties with a different partner every week might have a certain glamour, but no man in his sixties or seventies can sustain that kind of lifestyle – even if he were still able to attract casual partners (a big 'if'), his peers would regard him as a dirty old man, with no glamour whatsoever. Casual sex harms men too, though not as immediately, and not as obviously.

But casual sex harms women most of all. I realise that avoiding it will often be difficult, given the pressures of the twenty-first-century dating market, but, unless you are in the small minority of women who are exceptionally high in sociosexuality (in which case you will have scored 'zero' on my earlier list of questions), the risks of casual sex are going to outweigh the benefits.

Being alone with an unknown, horny man will always be somewhat dangerous for any woman, given the differences in size and strength. And although it's of course true that husbands and long-term boyfriends also commit domestic violence, that's no reason to do away with the vetting process altogether. It's better to date men that are already part of one's social network because, if they've developed a reputation for treating their girlfriends badly, you are likely to hear about this through mutual friends. When you date a stranger from the internet, the only person who can give you information about his sexual history is the man himself, and his account is unreliable. What's more, there is nothing stopping him from treating his date badly and then melting back into the night, having suffered no social consequences whatsoever. Mutual friends and acquaintances can punish bad behaviour. Dating apps can't.

The fact that a man wants to have sex with a woman *is not an indication* that he wants a relationship with her. Holding off on having sex for at least the first few months is therefore a good vetting strategy for several reasons. Firstly, it filters out the men who are just looking for a hook-up. Secondly, it gives a woman time to get to know a man before putting herself in a position of vulnerability. Thirdly, avoiding the emotional attachment that comes with a sexual relationship makes it easier to spot red flags. Free from the befuddling effects of hormones, it's possible to assess a new boyfriend's behaviour with clearer eyes.

One of the factors that acts against women in heterosexual dating is the gender gap in the personality trait that psychologists call 'agreeableness', colloquially more likely to be referred to as 'niceness'. It has long been known by researchers that, on average, women are much more agreeable than men. This sex difference could be a result of nature, or nurture, or a combination of both – it doesn't especially matter, at least not for my purposes here. The point is that there is a gap – and a substantial one – between men and women in this most crucial of traits.[42]

Agreeable people are more likely to put their own interests last and, against the evidence, more likely to think the best of people. I'm a very agreeable person, which means, for instance, that I tend to avoid interpersonal conflict and I'm terrible at negotiating pay. If you want to know how agreeable you are, you can search online for 'big five personality test' – it's a useful thing to know about yourself, because it can help to guide your behaviour. I now know that being excessively agreeable is my path of least resistance, so I make a conscious effort to be more assertive.

Agreeable people are particularly vulnerable to being taken advantage of by disagreeable people and, given that women are on average significantly more agreeable than men are, this has obvious relevance to sexual politics. So my advice to agreeable women assessing potential partners is not to ask yourself 'Would this man make a good boyfriend *for me*?', because doing so risks allowing your niceness to override your good sense. Ask yourself instead 'Would this man make a good *father to my children*?' – not because you necessarily intend to have children with this man, or indeed with anyone, but because agreeable people find it easier to prioritise the interests of people they love than to prioritise their own interests.

And if he wouldn't make a good father, don't have sex with him. It means that he isn't worthy of your trust.

Liberal feminism has valorised having sex 'like a man' as a route to women's liberation. But we will never be able to have sex like men, because we will never be men. There is an inherent asymmetry to heterosexuality that can't be overcome, despite the existence of modern contraception and other forms of technology that offer a brittle illusion of sameness. We can either accept that fact, and act accordingly, or we can keep sending young women out as cannon fodder in the battle against sexist double standards and then, when they return wounded, decry sexism all the louder. I'd also like to live in a world in which women can do whatever they want, without fear of what men might do to them. But we don't live in that world. Our present reality demands that both men and women accept the existence of the sexual asymmetry, even if that means curtailing our freedoms. And, unwelcome as that reality may be, we are obliged to describe it truthfully.

5

Consent Is Not Enough

In 2015, Andrew Norfolk, chief investigative reporter for *The Times*, gave a lecture on the four years he and his colleagues had spent reporting on child sexual abuse committed by gangs in British cities, including Rotherham, Rochdale, Telford and Oxford. He described the experiences of a victim whose case had stuck in his mind:

> One of the victims was a girl from Essex, but she'd been put into a children's home in Rotherham, and she was the only resident of that children's home . . . In two months in that home she'd gone missing fifteen times, for periods ranging from a day to a fortnight, and on one of those missing nights she'd been taken to a house, put blind drunk into a bedroom, and cars had started arriving from all across Greater Manchester. Men were queueing on the stairs and on the landing outside the bedroom and the jury heard that fifty men had had sex with that girl in one night. She was a child.[1]

At exactly the same time, on the other side of the Atlantic, Kacey Jordan's porn career was already under way. Aged eighteen, Jordan had starred in porn films, including *All Teens 3*,

Barely 18 38, *Barely Legal 80*, *Just Legal Babes 2* and *Don't Let Daddy Know 4*. Despite being legally an adult, Jordan looked unusually young – petite with slim hips and small breasts – meaning that she was still able to star convincingly in 'teen' porn into her early twenties. In her most famous scene, fifty-eight amateurs (that is, ordinary men) took turns to ejaculate over her naked, childlike body.

At the age of twenty-two, Jordan livestreamed a suicide attempt over YouTube. She is now attempting to rebuild her life. In a 2018 interview, she spoke about her many plastic surgeries: 'I wanted to reinvent myself . . . one of the reasons for the boob job was that the fetishists were into the idea of me being underage, because it's rare for a grown adult like me to have the body of a 14 year old. That was why I sold so much porn.'[2] Years on, Jordan is able to speak candidly about how naiveté and grinding poverty led her into the sex industry. As a younger woman, though, she took a very different view, insisting point blank that she was a consenting adult who was free to do as she wished. Having reached her eighteenth birthday, she was legally entitled to give this response. The victim of the Rotherham gang, still a child, was not.

For practical reasons, the age of consent has to serve as a legal bright line, separating statutory rape from consensual sex. There is no other way that the law could function. Although young people undoubtedly mature at different rates, and the transition from childhood to adulthood is, like night turning to day, a gradual process, we have to establish an arbitrary marker. At 11pm, she is a child; at midnight, she becomes an adult. That's how it has to be.

But we all know that in the real world that doesn't quite work. If we recoil from Norfolk's account of fifty men queuing up to sexually violate a teenage girl who had been abandoned by the state services tasked with protecting her, how can we then watch video of a young woman only a few years older, looking just as much like a child, being violated by *even more* men, without a similar response? The sore, torn orifices are the same. The exhaustion and disorientation are the same. The men aroused by using and discarding a young woman presented to them as a 'teen' are also much the same.

This chapter is about the predatory nature of the porn industry and its destructive effects on the people involved in it. It's also about the idea of sexual consent, because the only defence that the porn industry has, when presented with its hideous list of crimes, is its own version of the sexual liberation narrative: everyone is consenting, everyone is an adult, the women like it, and *who are you to say otherwise*?

Now, we might respond by pointing out that actually not everyone *is* an adult, and not everyone *is* consenting, in the narrow legal sense of the word, given the very many images of children and non-consenting adults that can be found even on the most mainstream porn platforms. But the industry and its defenders are quick to dismiss such examples as outliers, swivelling back to the 'happy hookers' who prop up its reputation. And as long as those women are old enough, (moderately) sane enough, and don't say 'no' at the crucial moment, then they reach the legal consent threshold and the industry can do with them what it likes.

But consent has more layers to it than that. There is the barest definition of the term on which we have to rely in a court of law – did she and could she say 'no'? – but there is also a thicker meaning. And here I'm afraid we're going to have to let go of seductively simple ideas about consent derived from liberal individualism. I'm going to argue that, although 'but she consented' may do as a legal defence, it is not a convincing *moral* defence.

The 'Queen of Porn'

People – particularly young women – will sometimes claim the ability to consent to some of the worst harms you can imagine. The victims of child grooming gangs are no exception. Although some do desperately seek out help, only to be turned away, it is far more common for girls to reject anyone who tries to intervene to stop the abuse. Sometimes they do this because they've been intimidated into silence, but more often it's a consequence of something far more troubling: they think that the adult men abusing them are their loving boyfriends.

This is what grooming does. It's the same state described by more old-fashioned terms such as 'brainwashing' and 'Stockholm syndrome' – a total loss of psychological independence. Think of the wife brutally beaten by her husband who then throws herself across his body when the police try to arrest him, something that domestic violence victims do *all the time*. Think of the dead-eyed followers of Charles Manson, killing on command and then walking beaming into the courtroom, marching in unison with the letter 'X' carved into their foreheads to mark them out as 'Manson's girls'. Branding, incidentally, is a detail that often recurs in accounts of this kind of all-consuming abuse. One of the victims of the Oxford grooming gang was branded with an 'M', the initial of her pimp. Similarly, in 1994, a man called Alan Wilson used a hot knife to burn an 'A' and a 'W' into his wife's buttocks, an act for which he was tried and later acquitted, thus producing *R* v. *Wilson*, a famous piece of English case law. Wilson claimed his wife was turned on by being branded like a cow. The wife refused to testify. The court believed the husband.

Some researchers believe that the grooming response is adaptive: a perfectly rational response to the threat of violence. The anthropologist Michelle Scalise Sugiyama, for instance, suggests that the capture of women during warfare was such a common event in human evolutionary history that it had important effects on our psychology.[3] The women who were able to integrate into their new communities were best placed to survive, meaning that those who were able to emotionally attach to their captors had a selection advantage over those who resisted.

Of course, men can be groomed too. The original event for which Stockholm syndrome is named – the taking of hostages at a Swedish bank – involved the capture of several men, who also formed an intense attachment to their captor. But it is a phenomenon we observe far more often in women – perhaps, as Scalise Sugiyama argues, because of our evolutionary history. Perhaps instead (or additionally) because women are more likely than men to find themselves in the sort of situation that most efficiently induces the response: intimate proximity to a violent man.

Looked at from one angle, grooming is just a particularly intense and blind form of love, an emotional attachment that is fundamentally irrational but no less important and meaningful for that. Many women who have been in an abusive relationship will describe the feeling of being hopelessly trapped in the emotional forcefield of their abuser – terrified, wretchedly unhappy, but also desperate to stay.

For some women, there is no distinction between the experience of domestic abuse and the experience of performing in porn. Linda Lovelace (real name Linda Boreman), star of the 1972 hardcore film *Deep Throat*, is perhaps the most famous example of a woman who entered porn literally, as she later detailed in her autobiography *Ordeal*, at gunpoint. Her first husband, Chuck Traynor, physically and emotionally abused her and coerced her into prostitution and, later, porn. Although it was widely known in the porn industry that Traynor was beating Boreman behind closed doors, no one seemed to mind ('She seemed to have a sado-masochistic relationship with Chuck', shrugged the director of *Deep Throat* in a later interview).

When *Deep Throat* became an international success, grossing over $600 million,[4] Boreman toured the UK, attending Ascot in a miniskirt, and during a visit to Stonehenge announced:

> To be honest with you, it makes me so mad that sex films are called obscene when other movies are so full of slaughter and rated so that kids can see them. What kids should learn is that sex is good, and then there wouldn't be so many neurotics in the world. I mean you're only here once, so enjoy life![5]

'Linda Lovelace' appeared to be a grateful beneficiary of sexual liberation. Only later did she reveal the truth of what was done to her and become a campaigner against the porn industry. She wrote in *Ordeal* of her experiences of performing in porn:

> They treated me like an inflatable plastic doll, picking me up and moving me here and there. They spread my legs this way and that, shoving their things at me and into me, they were playing musical chairs with parts of my body. I have never been so frightened and disgraced and humiliated in my life. I felt like garbage. I engaged in sex acts in pornography against my will to avoid being killed.[6]

This is a consistent pattern: women who have worked in porn will conform to the liberation narrative while they're still a part of the industry and share the dark side of their experiences only once they've left. And by then their images are out in the world, and there's no way of getting them back. Boreman wrote in 1980 that 'everyone that watches *Deep Throat* is watching me being raped.' Half a century on, people are still watching it.

And younger women are still experiencing the (now hugely expanded) porn industry in much the same way that Boreman did. Vanessa Belmond, for instance, spent seven years performing in porn, between the ages of eighteen and twenty-five. She is explicit about the cruelty of the industry: the racism she experienced as a black woman,[7] the financial exploitation, the prevalence of STDs, and the total lack of respect for the boundaries and wellbeing of porn performers, many of whom came away from scenes with injuries and became dependent on drugs and alcohol to numb the physical and emotional pain. Belmond is also open about her own youthful experiences of an eating disorder[8] alongside addictions to drugs[9] and porn use,[10] all of which contributed to her entering the industry in the hopes of becoming as glamorous, beautiful and desired as she imagined porn performers to be. She describes the exploitative nature of an industry that chews up and spits out young women when they arrive as teenagers, dreaming of money and fame:

> Here is the pattern I have seen over and over again in my 7 years in this industry: Girl gets into porn, shoots regularly for about 6 months to a year doing relatively tame sex scenes. Work starts to slow down, so girl decides to do more hardcore scenes (things like anal, multiple men etc.). Work slows down again. Girl now starts escorting and becomes 'open' to doing just about anything on camera to get work. Eventually, there is no company willing to shoot her and porn work is dried up. Girl usually has no work history and often no schooling, and now is essentially stuck with escorting, stripping, webcamming and any porn work she might be able to scrape up.[11]

But, much like Linda Boreman, when Belmond was still involved in the industry, she was the first to insist that she was simply expressing her sexual agency:

> One by one, all of my boundaries were crossed. Did I ever tell my fans that? Of course not! As far as they knew, I started doing anal because I 'wanted to try something new.' If you had asked

these fans, I did the most hardcore sex scenes because I 'got into porn to act out all of my fantasies on camera!'

I was just a 'sexual' young girl trying out all of the things she fantasized about! Right? I certainly wasn't a broken-down young woman doing what she had to do to make money in the sex industry. I wasn't a young woman whose self-worth had been completely destroyed to the point where she felt like nothing more than an object, a commodity. Noooo. I was a 'liberated,' 'sexually open,' 'party girl!'[12]

This transition into and out of the 'liberated' role also holds true for those few women who do make it in porn. Jenna Jameson, for instance, is still one of the most famous porn actresses in the world and, for a time, one of its most visible supporters, christened the 'Queen of Porn' in the media. In 2001, the Oxford Union invited Jameson to come to Oxford to argue against the proposition 'The house believes that porn is harmful'. Her side won the debate, 204 to 27.[13] But Jameson is now a vehement critic of the sex industry. In her autobiography *How to Make Love Like a Porn Star: A Cautionary Tale* she writes of shooting scenes with performers she found repulsive, the near constant physical pain and exhaustion resulting from a gruelling schedule, and all this in an industry filled with abusive men who take any opportunity to degrade the women they work with. Jameson left the sex industry in 2008 and has since become an outspoken conservative and anti-porn campaigner.[14]

The crimes of MindGeek

Jameson's campaigning fury is directed in particular at Pornhub, the tenth most visited website in the world, and she has lent her support to the American campaign group TraffickingHub, who have been developing a growing body of evidence that Pornhub knowingly hosts videos of children and sex trafficking victims being raped, as well as so-called revenge porn shared without the victim's consent.

The Internet Watch Foundation has so far confirmed 118 cases of children being sexually abused on Pornhub.[15] One fifteen-year-old girl who had been missing for a year was found after her mother was tipped off that her daughter was being featured in videos on Pornhub – fifty-eight such videos of her rape and abuse were discovered. Another girl, fourteen-year-old Rose Kalemba, was gang raped at knifepoint. Footage of the attack was posted on Pornhub and viewed more than 400,000 times. Kalemba contacted the site repeatedly over a period of six months, asking for the video to be removed, but with no success. Meanwhile, Pornhub continued to profit from the footage of her assault. You don't need to go to the 'dark web' in order to access this material – it's available on the biggest, most mainstream porn site in the world.

Globally, the porn industry is certainly worth many billions of US dollars, with some placing the figure as high as $97 billion. MindGeek, the giant of the porn world, operates nearly a hundred websites, including Pornhub, that in total consume more bandwidth than Twitter, Amazon or Facebook.[16] MindGeek's organisational structure is complex, with an elaborate system of companies scattered all over the world, including in tax havens such as Cyprus and Luxembourg. In 2009, then owner Fabian Thylmann was arrested on charges of tax evasion and consequently sold MindGeek to Feras Antoon and David Marmorstein Tassillo. For the last decade, these two men have managed to keep an astonishingly low profile – Antoon has only a brief Wikipedia mention, and Marmorstein Tassillo has none at all. Unlike figures such as Jack Dorsey, Jeff Bezos and Mark Zuckerberg, the senior executives of MindGeek are not household names, and they have thus far been able to keep out of the media spotlight, accumulating vast wealth without the burden of public accountability.

In December 2020, an article in the *New York Times* delivered a painful blow to MindGeek. Pulitzer Prize-winning
journalist Nicholas Kristof conducted an investigation into
the failure of Pornhub to remove sexual images of children
and non-consenting adults from its platform. The *New York
Times* is not only one of the most prestigious news outlets in
the world, it is also a liberal publication that rarely publishes
articles critical of the sex industry. Thus Kristof's piece could
not easily be dismissed by Pornhub's defenders as yet another
example of conservative prudishness, and his damning verdict
was all the more persuasive: '[The Pornhub] site is infested with
rape videos. It monetizes child rapes, revenge pornography,
spy cam videos of women showering, racist and misogynist
content, and footage of women being asphyxiated in plastic
bags. A search for "girls under18" (no space) or "14yo" leads in
each case to more than 100,000 videos.'[17]

The response was immediate. Mastercard and Visa both
announced that they would be ending the use of their cards on
Pornhub and, four days after the publication of Kristof's piece,
MindGeek announced that it would create a new team of mod-
erators to review and remove 'potentially illegal material', ban
downloads, and change its upload policies so that only veri-
fied users would be permitted to post videos.[18] Pornhub later
purged all existing videos from unverified users, reducing the
number of videos on its platform from 13 million to 4 million.[19]
This was by far the most significant crackdown in the site's
history.

It was also not enough. An ongoing legal case gives a taste
of the sort of shady practices MindGeek has been involved
with, and could yet continue to be involved with, despite the
introduction of its new safeguarding measures. GirlsDoPorn
was a porn production company, founded in 2009, whose
channel was at one point one of the twenty most popular on
Pornhub. These were not amateur videos posted by unverified users – GirlsDoPorn was a slick, professional company

that relied on an elaborate scam. It placed fake modelling adverts on Craigslist asking for young women aged eighteen to twenty-two to contact them. Those who responded were put in touch with other women paid to pretend they had had positive experiences working for the company as models. Some of the women were told part of the truth: that they would be obliged to have sex on camera. But none were told the whole truth: that the videos would be distributed online.

GirlsDoPorn producers lied to these women, telling them that the videos would be sold on DVD to private buyers on the other side of the world. They also lied about the filming process, telling them that they would be expected to have sex for only 30 minutes. Instead, filming lasted up to seven hours. The women were coerced into producing porn that was then distributed without their knowledge. Half of them were not even given the total sum of money promised by the producers.

Monica Evans was one of the women who responded to a fake modelling ad posted by GirlsDoPorn producers in 2013, just two months after her eighteenth birthday. She was flown out to California, where she was coerced into filming hours of rough intercourse. As she later told *Vice*: 'I was in so much pain. I didn't want to do it anymore and they said, "No, you signed a contract, it's only ten more minutes" . . . I was there for four or five hours. It was torture. Then they took me to the airport. I cried the whole plane ride home.'[20] A month later, the video was everywhere. It was linked to Monica's social media accounts, her family were sent screenshots, and her little sister was harassed. Monica emailed Pornhub asking them to take down her video, but she never heard back. She was admitted to a psychiatric hospital.

Monica was one of the young women who later gave evidence in a civil case brought by twenty-two victims of GirlsDoPorn. In January 2020, the plaintiffs were awarded $12.775 million in damages and, during the course of the case, criminal charges were also brought, including sex trafficking and producing sexual images of a child. Some of the people associated with GirlsDoPorn have been charged by American federal authorities. Two of those defendants – porn actor Ruben Andre Garcia and cameraman Theodore Wilfred Gyi – have pleaded guilty and await sentencing, while GirlsDoPorn co creator Michael James Pratt remains at large.[21]

Although this civil lawsuit was filed in June 2016, Pornhub did not remove the GirlsDoPorn channel until October 2019,[22] when criminal charges were brought. In December 2020, forty women involved with GirlsDoPorn filed a further lawsuit claiming that MindGeek knew about the company's sex trafficking as early as 2009, and definitely by 2016, but nevertheless continued to partner with GirlsDoPorn.[23] The lawsuit also alleges that, as recently as December 2020, MindGeek failed to remove GirlsDoPorn videos despite requests for removal by victims. At the time of writing, the lawsuit remains outstanding.[24]

Despite this kind of barely concealed malpractice, MindGeek continues to churn out profits for one simple reason: people keep watching. Some of the abuses of the porn industry are deliberately hidden from consumers, with porn performers paid to moan with pleasure as they clench with agony. But sometimes the abuse is obvious. Sometimes, in fact, the abuse is *the point*.

The format of the GirlsDoPorn videos dwelt on the coercion rather than concealing it. Typically filmed in hotel rooms and with minimal crew, the women were given money on camera and asked to read parts of their (misleading) contracts out loud. There was no pretence that these women were enthusiastic participants – their reluctance was intended to be sexy. And, based on the success of GirlsDoPorn over its eleven-year existence, porn consumers found the genre very sexy indeed: these videos were viewed over a billion times on sites owned by MindGeek.

The porn industry would not produce content depicting abuse unless there were a demand for it. There is a darkness within human sexuality – mostly, but not exclusively, within men – that might once have been kept within a fantasist's skull, but which porn now makes visible for all the world to see. The industry takes this cruel, quiet seed and makes it grow.

Limbic capitalism

In a 2020 survey of men across a range of Western European countries, respondents reported watching an average of 70 minutes of online porn a week, with 2 per cent watching more than 7 hours.[25] The average man, it seems, spends more time watching porn than he does showering.[26]

And yet not all men watch porn, even in younger cohorts: a 2019 survey commissioned by the BBC found that 23 per cent of UK men aged eighteen to twenty-five reported having *not* watched porn in the last month.[27] Porn use is not evenly distributed through the population but, rather, conforms to the Pareto distribution, with a minority of people accounting for the vast majority of consumption. It is these consumers who are chiefly responsible for allowing the porn industry to flourish, and yet they are also exploited by the industry in their own way.

A lot of porn consumers feel conflicted about their use. Dr Fiona Vera Grey, a research fellow at Durham University, has conducted research with both men and women about their experiences of using porn. A common emotional response among users she's heard from is a feeling of overwhelming arousal, followed abruptly by feelings of shame immediately after orgasm. Many users, Vera Grey reports, 'have an ethical conflict going on in terms of seeing material that they feel is pretty shit for women, but personally they're aroused by it. . . .

So they're masturbating to material and then afterwards they think "oh my God", and they push the computer away.'[28]

Sexual arousal suppresses our disgust response[29] for a straightforward biological reason: other people are potential sources of disease, but we have to get close to other people in order to reproduce. The natural disinclination towards intimacy with strangers is therefore disabled when we find those strangers sexually attractive. And the disgust response is very closely linked with moral intuition.[30] Put simply, we're not as good at making fine-tuned moral judgements when we're horny.

And porn sites are set up to arouse users as quickly as possible. Not only do thumbnails show the most explicit moments of a video – always the act of penetration, never the performers just sitting on a bed – the links to videos are also often animated and play automatically when the user hovers a cursor over them, or else when the site opens. As soon as a user arrives, their eyes (and sometimes ears) are immediately bombarded with intense sexual stimuli. This basic drive, as fundamental as hunger or thirst, can't be resisted through moral reasoning. It is an involuntary response that the porn industry has become very adept at provoking.

This kind of website design is a particularly disturbing example of what Professor David Courtwright has called 'limbic capitalism', that is, a 'technologically advanced but socially regressive business system in which global industries, often with the help of complicit governments and criminal organizations, encourage excessive consumption and addiction. They do so by targeting the limbic system, the part of the brain responsible for feeling.'[31] Limbic capitalism is the reason why the most successful apps are brightly coloured like fresh fruit and glint like fresh water. Our primitive brains helplessly seek out the stimuli that we have evolved to be attracted to because responding to those stimuli gave our ancestors a survival advantage. Purveyors of limbic capitalism have become wise to these instincts and have learned over time how best to capture them.

Porn is to sex as McDonald's is to food. These two capitalist enterprises take our natural appetites, pluck out the most compulsive and addictive elements, strip away anything truly nutritious, and then encourage us to consume more and more. Both products are examples of superstimuli: exaggerated versions of naturally occurring stimuli that tap into an evolved longing for nourishment, excitement and pleasure but do so in a maladaptive way, fooling the consumer into gorging on a product that initially feels good but in the long term does them harm.

When faced with such temptations, we human beings are not all that much more sophisticated than the Australian jewel beetle (*Julodimorpha bakewelli*), a glossy, golden-coloured beetle around 4 cm long. In 1981, a pair of insect specialists observed a male jewel beetle attempting to mate with a discarded beer bottle (known in Australian slang as a 'stubbie'). Upon further investigation, they found that male jewel beetles were not only frequently mistaking stubbies for females of their species, they *actually preferred* the stubbies, ignoring potential mates in order to hump the glass bottles because these bits of litter were *more* glossy and *more* golden than the female jewel beetles, and thus more sexually exciting to the males.[32]

Porn provides much the same attraction, offering bigger breasts and bigger dicks than those encountered 'in the wild', and thus also offering more excitement. The impending arrival of realistic sex robots on the market is likely to intensify this superstimuli effect still further. The evolutionary biologist Diana Fleischman writes of the malign impact of these new pieces of technology on their purchasers:

> The cues a sex robot would provide to the evolved psychology of a previously disgruntled teenager would be 'you're achieving incredible mating success and status by staying at home and

playing video games, keep at it!' ... Video games and social
media already undermine the native psychological mecha-
nisms that make us work towards status – they supply more
immediate rewards and take far less effort than anything we
work towards out in the real world. Sex robots are only going
to make that worse, especially for young men.[33]

Why bother getting a job, going to the gym, or maintaining
your personal hygiene if your sex robot doesn't care either
way? If a sterile piece of plastic can keep a young man sexually
sated, he doesn't need to go out and meet real women. Of
course, he will never acquire a spouse or children and will
be left in the end with only his sex robot for companionship.
But he will arrive at that lonely state having been emotionally
cushioned by the reliable dopamine hit won from playing the
sexual equivalent of a slot machine game over and over again.

Even without access to sex robots, some men are already
prioritising watching porn over pursuing relationships with
real partners. As we'll see in chapter 7, one perverse feature
of the twenty-first-century dating market is that the average
young person is now having sex less often than their parents
and grandparents once did, and there is an increasingly large
and frustrated population of men who remain virgins into
their twenties and beyond. This subset of men is particularly
vulnerable to the purveyors of limbic capitalism.

The 2 per cent of Western European men who report watching more than 7 hours of porn a week are not a healthy and
happy group, and nor are the men whose porn use may be less
time-consuming but is nevertheless personally destructive. The
continuing influence of the NoFap movement is a testament
to the sexual dissatisfaction that often comes with porn use.
Founded in 2011 by the American web developer Alexander
Rhodes, NoFap encourages followers to give up both porn and
masturbation ('fap' being slang derived from the sound of a
man pleasuring himself). Followers – overwhelmingly male

– are offered freedom from the addictive power of porn and the consequent sexual impairment that has skyrocketed within the last twenty years, with erectile dysfunction now affecting between 14 and 35 per cent of young men, in contrast to perhaps 2 or 3 per cent at the beginning of this century.[34]

Members of the NoFap subreddit sometimes write of masturbating so often that they give themselves painful abrasions, and many report suffering from 'death grip syndrome', a quasi-medical term used to describe the loss of sensation that can sometimes result from masturbating too aggressively. Sufferers report finding it difficult or impossible to reach orgasm during sex with another person, partly because of physical desensitisation and partly because of the psychological effect of porn use. Even if they are motivated to seek out sex with a real person, psychological death grip may mean that they cannot become aroused by someone whose body isn't exactly like that of a porn star. Compulsive porn users expose themselves to so much sexual stimulation that they literally become impotent.

The American actor and athlete Terry Crews is now an advocate of the NoFap movement, having publicly spoken about his own struggle with porn addiction: 'Some people say, "Hey, man . . . you can't really be addicted to pornography." But I'm gonna tell you something . . . It changes the way you think about people. People become objects. People become body parts; they become things to be used rather than people to be loved.'[35] Crews is handsome, rich and successful. He is also a husband and father of five. Nevertheless, he found himself neglecting his wife and watching porn instead, like an Australian jewel beetle choosing an inert object over a real, living mate. Such is the power that porn has over some users.

The feminists who criticised porn in the 1970s and 1980s got a lot right, correctly predicting the industry's direction of travel. The infamous June 1978 cover of *Hustler* magazine, depicting a woman's body being pulped in a meat grinder, now looks almost tame compared to the images of grotesque sexual violence that are available, not only on mainstream porn sites but also on social media platforms marketed as suitable for children.

But something that this generation of feminists didn't predict was the paradoxical effect that pornification would have on sexual behaviour at the population level. On the one hand, we have a sexual script that has become increasingly aggressive and loveless. But, on the other, we have a group of men who are so stupefied by porn that they are (sometimes permanently) impaired in their ability to have sexual relationships with real people. Put simply, the porn generation are having *less sex*, and the sex they are having *is also worse*: less intimate, less satisfying and less meaningful.

Logging off

We are rapidly entering a world in which tech dominates the most intimate parts of our lives, and this tech is designed by corporations whose sole interest is profit making. The writer Venkatesh Rao describes this as a world in which 'you either tell robots what to do, or are told by robots what to do' – you live either above the algorithm, or below it.[36] The porn industry is a particularly unpleasant example of this creeping domination, since all but a tiny number of us are to be found below the algorithm.

There are a few people in the porn industry who are unambiguously villainous – the executives of MindGeek, who are found determinedly above the algorithm, do not provoke any sympathy in me – but there are many more people below the algorithm whose moral status is harder to define. In particular, porn users, who are both the drivers of the industry and also its victims: not as victimised as the performers, of course, but victimised nonetheless. They are caught up in a form of limbic capitalism that takes our most basic instincts and corrupts them in the pursuit of profit. You cannot criticise capitalism without also criticising its most debased offspring, the porn industry, which destroys its workers and its consumers alike.

And yet most anti-capitalists prefer to look away. In fact, the most committed defences of porn come nowadays from self-described 'sex-positive' leftists who claim that any criticism of the *industry* must necessarily be a criticism of its *workers* (funnily enough, they do not make the same defence of industries that rely on sweatshop labour). These apologists are aided, in part, by the efforts of the industry to sanitise its practices. Pornhub, for instance, runs a smoke and mirrors exercise it calls 'Pornhub Cares', with campaigns against plastic pollution and the destruction of bee and giant panda habitats ('Pornhub is calling on our community to help get pandas in the mood. We're making panda style porn!')

But a far more effective counter to any criticism of the industry is the sexual liberation narrative, always available to comfort any porn user who feels a squirm of discomfort at what they're funding. Kacey Jordan, Jenna Jameson, Vanessa Belmond and Linda Lovelace all gave some version of this narrative at the height of their fame, responding to anyone who asked with a dismissive 'of course I'm consenting.' All of these women later changed their minds, after the porn industry had had its fill of them, and after the damage to their bodies and psyches had already been done.

Taking a woman at her word when she says 'of course I'm consenting' is appealing because it's easy. It doesn't require us to look too closely at the reality of the porn industry or to think too deeply about the extent to which we are all – whether as a consequence of youth, or trauma, or credulousness, or some murky combination of all three – capable of hurting or even destroying ourselves. You can do terrible and lasting harm to a 'consenting adult' who is begging you for more.

Some feminists place their faith in so-called ethical porn, but this hypothetical product serves only to distract from the reality of how the porn industry really operates. For one thing, porn marketed as 'ethical' makes up such a tiny and unpopular proportion of the market that focusing on it is like, as feminist writer Sarah Ditum has put it, 'putting a chicken in your back garden and claiming you've fixed factory farming.'[37] For another, whatever 'ethical' label may be stuck on a video, you cannot look at it and know for sure that the people in it were truly happy to be there. Just as importantly, you cannot look at a video and know if the people in it are *still happy* that their images are out in the world. Linda Lovelace was an enthusiastic defender of the porn industry during her promotion of *Deep Throat*: it was only years later that she said that viewers were 'watching me being raped'.

And even aside from the conditions of its production, the product itself will always have a damaging effect on the consumer's sexuality. The feminist critic Laura Mulvey has used the phrase 'the invisible guest' to describe the role of the viewer who looks on at the events of a film, forgotten in the corner of the room.[38] The role of the porn viewer should be understood as that of an invisible voyeur. Porn trains the mind to regard sex as a spectator sport, to be enjoyed alone and in front of a screen. It removes love and mutuality from sex, turning human beings – as Terry Crews has put it – 'into body parts'.

This is one of those rare problems that has such a blindingly simple solution: opt out. Regardless of whether the state regulates the porn industry – as I believe it ought to – the individual maintains absolute control over whether or not he or she directly contributes to it. There is no good reason to use porn. Giving it up costs the consumer nothing. It is easier by far than giving up factory-farmed meat or products made by sweatshop labour because, although we all need to eat and clothe ourselves, not a single one of us needs to watch porn ever again. The sexual liberation narrative tells you to keep going; I'm telling you that you have an obligation to stop.

6

Violence Is Not Love

One of the pleasurable things about BDSM, from a business perspective, is that it so often demands kit. The British high-street retailer Ann Summers currently offers a six-piece 'bondage set' for £60, a starter pack which includes a flogger, blindfold, ball gag, ankle cuffs, handcuffs and rope. To this could be added dozens of other items from the Ann Summers BDSM range, from multi-chain nipple clamps (£15) to basic hog ties (£10).

Many of these products feature *Fifty Shades of Grey* branding, the novel and film franchise having provided a golden opportunity for Ann Summers to diversify its range. In 2017, the flagship store at London's Marble Arch invited customers to visit a basement room – 'The Red Room' – devoted to all things *Fifty Shades*. There could be found a bondage dog crate, butt plugs with fluffy tails, a penis cage, and a £10,000 vibrator that came complete with matching cufflinks.[1] Who knew that sexual liberation could be so profitable?

This marketing wheeze was entirely in keeping with the spirit of the *Fifty Shades* franchise, which eroticises wealth just as much as it eroticises sexual dominance. Christian Grey, the troubled romantic hero, is charming, handsome, and knows his way around a fluffy butt plug. He is also a billionaire, and the victim of his affections, Anastasia, is wooed just as much by his Airbus EC130 helicopter as she is by the sex dungeon that he calls his 'Red Room'. Of course, take away all of these distractions, and what Christian Grey really undertakes is just common-or-garden domestic abuse. He becomes obsessed with a much younger, virginal woman. He wins her over by bombarding her with attention. He controls her every move, from what she wears to who she spends time with. He even dictates what she's allowed to eat.

And here's the troubling thing: a lot of women loved it. Not all women – personally, I'm unmoved by Christian Grey's charms, as are most of the friends I've spoken to – but, for a sizeable minority, the combination of domestic abuse and ostentatious wealth proved highly arousing and therefore highly lucrative – for the author E. L. James herself, for publishers, for filmmakers and for retailers of BDSM gear, including Ann Summers.

Radical feminists have historically explained this disturbing form of arousal as the product solely of socialisation, imbibed from a culture that celebrates female submission and male domination. Although there is some truth to this idea, the radical feminist analysis doesn't fully explain the popularity of BDSM among the women who bought *Fifty Shades*. The sad truth is that a minority of women do find BDSM very sexy, and you do not have to go far to find such women publicly defending the practice as an expression of their sexual agency. To my mind, a more plausible (and more distressing) explanation for this behaviour has to include a recognition that some women may be primed to find Christian Grey's abusive behaviour arousing – and that priming is a consequence not only of culture but also of biology.

The idea of possessiveness

In chapter 2, we confronted the fact that there are important average differences between men and women when it comes to sexuality. One striking feature of typical female sexuality is a preoccupation with partners' displays of emotional loyalty. This is a logical consequence of the fact that a pregnant and nursing woman is astonishingly vulnerable, and she and her baby are more likely to survive if she has a committed and well-resourced mate. A man may demonstrate his suitability for the role in various ways, for instance by buying gifts, lavishing his mate with attention, and showing kindness towards children.

He can also show his commitment in more unpleasant ways. Christian Grey is a violent, controlling brute, but his obsessive behaviour towards Anastasia does at least demonstrate his unwavering commitment to her. *Fifty Shades* adds a whips-and-chains aesthetic, but many older romance novels are centred on much the same dynamic: the strong handsome man who falls head over heels in love with the heroine and will do anything to have her, up to and including being violent.

Next time you're in your local library, have a look at the covers and blurbs of some Mills & Boon novels, written for an older and more traditionalist audience than *Fifty Shades*. Invariably the heroes are portrayed as big and muscly and are either high-status professionals (surgeons, say) or adventurous vagabonds (pirates or highwaymen). There is variation within the romance genre, and heroes may be more or less aggressive depending on the particular book, but one theme remains consistent: the consumers of women's erotic fiction have never been turned on by a man who plays hard to get, wavers in his interest, or is distracted by the attentions of other women. Long before *Fifty Shades* came along, what these readers were aroused by is the fantasy of a man who is *really into them*, often obsessively so.

Sometimes that desire for undivided attention favours the gentle giant who is loving and tender towards women, children and kittens. But a woman's perfectly rational desire for a loyal mate can also sometimes be hijacked by the likes of Christian Grey, who is undoubtedly committed to Anastasia but is also controlling and dangerous.

The tragedy is that, while the fictional Christian Grey may be faithful to Anastasia, his real life counterpart often isn't. It's easy enough for an inexperienced or overly trusting woman to confuse jealousy for fidelity and so be drawn to the aggressive heroes of erotic fiction. But, in reality, the two character traits do not necessarily go hand in hand.

The conservative writer and psychiatrist Theodore Dalrymple has never been one for repeating feminist pieties, which in this instance makes his analysis of the jealousy dynamic more candid. When working at a hospital in a deprived area of Birmingham, England, Dalrymple often encountered both the victims and the perpetrators of domestic abuse, and he writes about his patients' experiences with no effort to mince his words:

> The great majority of the jealous men I meet are flagrantly unfaithful to the object of their supposed affections, and some keep other women in the same jealous subjection elsewhere in the city and even 100 miles away. They have no compunction about cuckolding other men and actually delight in doing so as a means of boosting their own fragile egos. As a result, they imagine that all other men are their rivals: for rivalry is a reciprocal relationship. Thus a mere glance in a pub directed at a man's girlfriend is sufficient to start a fight not only between the girl and her lover but, even before that, between the two men.[2]

As for the women who become involved with such men, Dalrymple writes of a self-harming instinct which is not often acknowledged among feminists but is likely to be familiar to anyone who has ever worked with victims of domestic abuse:

> But why does the woman not leave the man as soon as he manifests his violence? It is because, perversely, violence is the only token she has of his commitment to her. Just as he wants the exclusive sexual possession of her, she wants a permanent relationship with him. She imagines – falsely – that a punch in the face or a hand round the throat is at least a sign of his continued interest in her, the only sign other than sexual intercourse she is ever likely to receive in that regard. In the absence of a marriage ceremony, a black eye is his promissory note to love, honour, cherish, and protect.[3]

In this chapter, I'm going to argue that BDSM is simply a ritualised and newly legitimised version of a toxic dynamic that is all too common between men and women. Although the sexual domination of 'subs' by 'doms' may have been given a counter-cultural gloss in recent decades, it is in fact as old as the hills. As we will see, BDSM enthusiasts have worked hard to present their sexual interest as a means of subverting the status quo, but in fact it is nothing of the sort. The mainstreaming of BDSM has, firstly, served to protect the interests of men who want to beat up women and avoid being punished for it, and, secondly, it has made a lot of money for the porn industry and for manufacturers of tacky leatherette clothing. In other words, BDSM is good for abusive men and good for capital. It subverts nothing.

The popular representation of BDSM often focuses on a very particular and unusual relationship in which a wealthy businessman pays a female dominatrix for regular whippings. These relationships do exist, and their amusingly counter-intuitive dynamics make them attractive to screenwriters and journalists. But they are not typical.

Most submissives ('subs') are female and most dominants ('doms') are male. One 2013 study[4] of participants in a BDSM online forum found that only 34 per cent of men consistently preferred the sub position, while an even smaller proportion of women – 8 per cent – identified as doms. The same study found that doms tended to be low in the agreeableness personality trait, meaning that they were assertive and demanding. Subs, in contrast, tended to be more agreeable than average, meaning that they were eager to please. These findings call into question the idea that people are drawn to BDSM roles that go against their normal dispositions – in fact, the opposite seems to be true. Most of the time, doms remain doms outside of the bedroom (or sex dungeon), and subs remain subs. In the real world, BDSM does not defy the sexual domination of women by men – rather, *it reinforces it*.

The Sutcliffean woman

But this is not, I regret to say, the dominant feminist view in the twenty-first century. It was not even the unanimous view in the 1970s, when radical feminism was riding high. In the influential text *The Sadeian Woman*, for instance, published in 1978, Angela Carter attempted a literary deconstruction of the writings of the grandfather of BDSM: the Marquis de Sade, the French aristocrat for whom 'sadism' is named. Immersed in the psychoanalytic style that was fashionable at the time, Carter identified in Sade's work a kind of proto-feminism, referring to 'the pornographer' – of which Sade is the pre-eminent example – as an 'unconscious ally' to women, 'because he begins to approach some kind of emblematic truth.'[5] *The Sadeian Woman* is part of a long, sorry history of feminists prioritising their own intellectual masturbation over their obligation to defend the interests of women and girls.

Carter is not alone in venerating Sade, and in the years since the publication of *The Sadeian Woman* she has been joined by many other sex-positive feminists keen to reclaim BDSM for women. There are also plenty of men who have historically enjoyed Sade's work. Flaubert and Baudelaire, for instance, rediscovered his writings in the nineteenth century and, in the 1920s, Surrealists including Man Ray, André Breton, and Dali were attracted to Sade's demand for absolute sexual freedom.[6]

These renegades fell well outside of the mainstream in their own time and, in fact, struggled to get hold of copies of Sade's books, since they were banned in France until 1957.[7] But in the 1960s Sade's work became widely available and acquired a new glamour. Gonzague Saint Bris, the author of a recent biography of Sade, sees his influence in the sexual revolution of the 1960s.[8] As a twenty-year-old during the May 1968 student riots in Paris, Saint Bris recalls, 'I looked at all the placards, reading "It is Forbidden to Forbid," and "Do Whatever You Desire." I suddenly understood that our revolutionary phrases were actually from Sade. I began to see a phantom wearing his powdered wig standing on the barricades beside me!'[9]

Sade maintains a chic reputation in some quarters today, so much so that one of the marquis's living descendants, the Count de Sade, has been able to capitalise on the family name to produce a line of *Maison de Sade* luxury goods, including wine, scented candles, and – in honour of the bicentennial of his death – a bust of the marquis that retailed for US$5,700.[10] In that year, several prestigious Parisian museums put on exhibitions to commemorate Sade's life and work.[11] As far as I can tell, all of these eminent defenders of Sade know full well what he got up to in real life – the fact that he imprisoned, raped and tortured many prostituted women and servants, including several children, and that these victims most certainly did not consent to what was done to them and told the authorities as much after they had escaped.

From the age of thirty-seven, Sade spent much of his life in prison and was then able to perpetrate his violent fantasies only in print. In his magnum opus, *120 Days of Sodom*, Sade fantasises about horror upon misogynist horror. If he had been free to, it seems likely that his violent sexual adventures and murderous fantasies would ultimately have escalated to actual murder, and his victims would probably have been found among the same poor women and children he persecuted in the years before his imprisonment. Sade's eighteenth-century setting may give him an air of otherness, but he was really no different from any modern sex offender with a taste for torture and mutilation. Angela Carter might as well have penned a hymn to the Yorkshire Ripper and called it *The Sutcliffean Woman*.

Feminists such as Carter may have been fooled by Sade's dark mystique, but Andrea Dworkin was not. Writing in 1979, Dworkin saw Sade for what he was – an aristocratic psychopath who used his sex, wealth and power to gain access to the bodies of the poor:

> Those leftists who champion Sade might do well to remember that prerevolutionary France was filled with starving people. The feudal system was both cruel and crude. The rights of the aristocracy to the labor and bodies of the poor were unchallenged and not challengeable. The tyranny of class was absolute. The poor sold what they could, including themselves, to survive. Sade learned and upheld the ethic of his class.[12]

On Easter Sunday in 1768, Sade came upon one of his victims, a widow called Rose Keller, when she was begging on the streets of Paris, having been made destitute after her husband's death. He offered her work as a housekeeper and she went with Sade to his house, where he whipped and badly injured her. Keller later said that she believed Sade would kill her, and when she managed to escape from his house she ran half naked and in terror until she found refuge with some local women, who alerted the police.[13]

It is no coincidence that Keller was poor. It is no coincidence that Sade was able to avoid imprisonment by paying her off. It is no coincidence that he abducted her on Easter Sunday, since Sade was aroused almost as much by blasphemy as he was by misogyny, and this anti-clerical instinct has done much to increase his reputation among atheist intellectuals of the modern era. To such intellectuals, Sade's victims are made invisible – dismissed as mere servants and whores, now long dead – and his rebellion against the conservative mores of his time is valorised. Dworkin had it right when she wrote of the 'freedom' that Sade represents to his fans: 'Sade suffered because he did what you want to do; he was imprisoned as you might be imprisoned. The "you" is masculine. The freedom Sade is credited with demanding is freedom as men conceive it.'[14]

Choking

If only Dworkin's analysis had won out. Unfortunately, among most twenty-first-century feminists, Carter is triumphant. The masculine freedom represented by Sade – the freedom to hurt, degrade and humiliate – is available to sample by both men and women in our newly liberated sexual culture, but with just one change: unlike Sade, today's sadists are obliged to seek consent. And that, we're told, makes all the difference.

Roxane Gay, for instance, in her bestselling book *Bad Feminist*, offers a directive that sounds simple enough:

> For people who enjoy BDSM, there's this thing called consent, which should always exist in human interactions, but which is exceedingly important when you entrust your body and mind to someone else in such ways. You can say, 'I want you to

hurt me,' or 'I want you to humiliate me,' or 'I want you to dominate me,' and someone else will do so. But, and this is important, when you say, in some form or fashion, stop, the pain or humiliation or domination stops, no questions asked.[15]

Gay is personally a fan of BDSM and, in a recent anthology of short stories on the theme, she writes about a man who takes pleasure in slapping his wife, strangling her with a belt, and scarring her back with a razor blade.[16] By the end of the story we discover that the man is in fact transgender, which supposedly transforms the nature of the couple's abusive sex.

Of all of the sex acts associated with BDSM, strangulation is currently the most fashionable and also the most gendered. In porn, men strangle men, men strangle women, but women are very rarely the ones doing the strangling. Strangulation *outside of sex* is also gendered, with the vast majority of victims being female and the vast majority of perpetrators being male. One study in San Diego found that, of 300 forensic records reporting strangulation, 298 involved a man strangling a woman. And it is a crime that is very often suffered by victims of domestic violence, most of whom are women.

The UK domestic abuse charity Refuge reports that 48 per cent of women using their services report having been strangled, choked or suffocated, and women who have previously been strangled by their partners are eight times more likely to be killed by them, often by strangulation, since this is the second most common method of murder used by men against women in the UK.[17] Scrolling through 'choking' porn and seeing image after image of men with their hands around women's throats, anyone not trained in the ideology of liberal feminism would be forgiven for seeing nothing more than bog-standard male violence against women – the kind of violence that feminists are supposed to be united against.

The trend for sexual strangulation has not confined itself to porn. Research conducted by ComRes in 2019 found that over half of eighteen- to 24-year-old UK women reported having been strangled by their partners during sex, compared with 23 per cent of women in the oldest age group surveyed, aged thirty-five to thirty-nine.[18] Many of these respondents reported that this experience had been unwanted and frightening, but others reported that they had consented to it, or even invited it.

And here lies the complication, because you don't have to look hard to find women who say they love being strangled, and these willing women – girls, really, many of them – are held up as mascots by those who defend the fashion for sexual strangulation. The argument from liberal feminists such as Roxane Gay is that, since there are some women who enjoy being strangled, it is wrong to condemn strangulation per se – it is only non-consensual strangulation that deserves our condemnation. It is exactly the same argument that we have come across earlier in this book: with consent, anything goes.

In July 2020, for instance, *Men's Health* magazine ran a feature titled 'Breath play is a popular form of BDSM. Here's how to do it safely',[19] and when Member of Parliament Laura Farris criticised the article for being anti-feminist, she was met with a huge backlash on Twitter, largely from young women who insisted that consensual strangulation can be a harmless form of kink. Gigi Engle, a sex writer for *Men's Health*, joined Farris's critics in tweeting 'Nope. Laura, sweetie, choking can be a very fun Sex act when done safely and consenually [sic].'[20]

But Engle is wrong on this. An alarming study from 2020 reveals the range of injuries that can be caused by non-fatal strangulation, including cardiac arrest, stroke, miscarriage, incontinence, speech disorders, seizures, paralysis, and other forms of long-term brain injury.[21] Although it takes several minutes to actually kill someone by strangulation, unconsciousness or 'choking out' can occur within seconds and always indicates at least a mild brain injury. Dr Helen Bichard, the lead author of the study, reports that the injuries caused by strangulation may not be visible to the naked eye, or may only become evident hours or days after the attack, meaning that they are far less obvious than injuries such as wounds or broken bones, and so may be missed during a police investigation.

Bichard rejects on medical grounds the idea that strangulation can ever be done safely, describing this as an urban myth: 'I cannot see a way of safely holding a neck so that you wouldn't be pressing on any fragile structures.'[22] And, given the possible consequences of strangulation, until recently only partially understood, Bichard argues that the vast majority of laypeople are not capable of giving truly informed consent to it.

The *Men's Health* piece got something else wrong, too, by suggesting that strangulation is arousing primarily because 'cutting off the brain's oxygen supply can cause feelings of lightheadedness.' This bio-medical attempt to explain the fashion for sexual strangulation is quite common and is appealing in its simplicity, but it leaves out a crucial factor. It is certainly true that a fetish for auto-erotic asphyxiation is attractive to some *men*, and, every now and again, men with a sexual interest in strangulation will be found dead, having accidentally killed themselves during a misjudged masturbation session.[23]

But a fetish for strangling *oneself* is vanishingly rare among women, so much so that I have not been able to find a single case in the UK of a woman accidentally killing herself during an auto-erotic asphyxiation attempt gone wrong, with the notable exception of 21-year-old Hope Barden, who died in 2019, having been paid to hang herself on webcam by Jerome Danger, a sexual sadist obsessed with extreme porn.[24]

If it is really true that women are drawn to strangulation because of the high induced by oxygen deprivation, then why is it that women are not strangling themselves alone, but instead are asking their male partners to do it to them? The answer is straightforward enough: because these women are not getting off on the lack of oxygen, but instead on the power play.

Sadly, images of strangulation shared or liked by women on social media, discussions between women on platforms such as Reddit and Twitter, and testimony that I've heard directly from many young women all suggest that many of the women who seek out strangulation have a very particular – and very misguided – understanding of what strangulation *means* when men do it to them during sex.

To put it bluntly, many of these women are as deluded as the victim of domestic violence, described by Theodore Dalrymple earlier in this chapter, who 'imagines – falsely – that a punch in the face or a hand round the throat is at least a sign of his continued interest in her.' They think strangulation indicates a man's love, passion and desire for them. More often than not, it indicates none of these things, but, in a culture in which the differences between male and female sexuality are routinely denied, particularly by liberal feminists, it shouldn't surprise us that many of these young women take the lead from erotic fiction such as *Fifty Shades* and misinterpret aggression from their male partners as a sign of passion, not realising that real-life Christian Greys usually have no interest whatsoever in the wellbeing of the women they (to use a nasty piece of porn terminology) 'hatefuck'.

Dr Scott Hampton is a clinical psychologist and director of Ending the Violence, an American organisation committed to addressing gender-based violence. Hampton has spent more than thirty years running offender treatment programmes inside American prisons and has collected a long and dispiriting series of accounts from domestic violence perpetrators, some of whom discuss their reasons for strangling their partners during sex.[25] These accounts provide a far more candid insight into the motivations of men who strangle women than any erotic fiction ever could.

Hampton's patients do not strangle out of love or out of any desire to heighten their partner's pleasure. They do it to show how powerful they are: 'No better way to get her full attention, especially when she realizes I could end her life in a snap, literally', says one man. 'The look of terror in her face is such a rush. She can't help but look at you. You're right there', says another. For a man with a fragile ego, strangulation can be appealing as a way of displaying absolute strength and dominance over a woman who is then forced to look right into his eyes.

We Can't Consent to This

Even if you accept the liberal feminist claim that it is possible for someone to truly and meaningfully consent to being strangled by their sexual partner, you are still faced with the problem of how the law is supposed to differentiate between consensual and non-consensual instances of sexual violence. *Emmett*, a piece of English case law from 1999, highlights the difficulty. The case involved a man who poured lighter fluid over his partner's breasts and then set her alight, causing third-degree burns. The woman visited her GP for treatment of the injury, and the GP – suspecting domestic violence – took the unusual step of violating patient–doctor confidentiality by making a report to the police. The woman refused to give evidence when the case came to court, and her partner insisted that she had consented to everything that he did.

What is the court to do, in such a case? As Jonathan Herring, professor of law at the University of Oxford, explains:

> In cases where a domestic abuser is charged with assaulting their partner where there are proven injuries, explaining the injuries as the results of consensual sadomasochism is one of the few defences available to them and if the victim is too scared to give evidence, then it will be a hard defence for the prosecution to rebut.[26]

Even if the victim in *Emmett* had been willing to give evidence and had supported her partner's account, the court might still have been unsure as to whether her consent was truly free, since, as Herring points out, 'there are uncomfortable links between the cases where an abuser has sought to control his victim and every aspect of her life, and cases where a BDSM master has sought control of his slave.'[27] From the outside, a consensual BDSM relationship and an abusive relationship look exactly the same, and so if a sub is injured or killed during a sexual encounter, and her dom claims it was an accident, how exactly are the courts supposed to tell the difference?

This is not a theoretical problem. The We Can't Consent to This campaign, which I've worked on, has documented sixty-seven cases in the UK in which people have been killed and their killers have claimed that their deaths were the result of a sex game 'gone wrong'. All suspects in these killings have so far been male, and sixty of those killed have been female. Most of the victims died from strangulation, although a significant minority suffered serious genital trauma. Most of the victims were the wives or girlfriends of perpetrators, and often there was evidence of domestic abuse. Other women had only met the perpetrators that day, and a large number of victims were involved in the sex trade.

There are two striking trends in the data we've collected. Firstly, the number of rough sex cases has increased significantly since the turn of this century; secondly, defendants who rely on this defence have increasingly been meeting with success, with roughly half of these homicide cases now ending without a conviction for murder. Put differently, within the last two decades, courts have become much more willing to believe defendants when they claim that their victims died because they literally 'asked for it'.

Some of the sentences handed down in these cases have been shockingly light. For instance, three cases in 2018 resulted in a manslaughter conviction after defendants relied on a 'rough sex defence' when charged with murder. John Broadhurst was sentenced to 3 years 8 months when his girlfriend Natalie Connolly died in his home from a combination of intoxication and vaginal haemorrhage, having been violently penetrated by Broadhurst with a bottle of carpet cleaner.[28] Jason Gaskell was sentenced to 6 years when he slit the throat of Laura Huteson during sex, using a knife he kept under his pillow.[29] And Mark Bruce was also sentenced to six years after he picked up a seriously drunk Chloe Miazek from a bus stop, took her back to his home, and strangled her to death (Bruce's barrister said in court that 'it would seem to be a complete coincidence that Mr Bruce met another person who shared his interest in that particular activity').[30]

Feminists in other parts of the world have also documented a rise in the use of the rough sex defence, with similar cases found in Canada,[31] Italy,[32] Russia,[33] Mexico,[34] Germany[35] and the United States.[36] The increasing popularity and success of the 'rough sex defence' internationally seems to be a result of the fact that courts are increasingly willing to believe that women not only consent to, but *actually seek out*, the kind of violence that can prove lethal. The phenomenon thus provides compelling evidence of the large-scale consequences of the normalisation of BDSM.

This normalisation is glaringly obvious online, where BDSM content, particularly content featuring strangulation, has migrated from niche porn sites to mainstream porn sites, and now to social media, including platforms that advertise themselves as suitable for children aged thirteen and over. On Instagram, there are tens of thousands of sexualised choking images available with hashtags such as #chokeme, #chokeher, #neckfetish, #breathplay and #chokeherout. On Pinterest there are images of children being gripped by the throat. One picture on Tumblr showed a bed with rose petals spelling out the words 'bruise my oesophagus'.[37] On these platforms, strangulation of women is presented as loving, sexy, stylish, desirable and sometimes amusing, and images are almost always taken from the perspective of the person doing the strangling.

You do not have to go searching for these images. If you are exposed to mainstream porn, or even just to mainstream social media, you are very likely to come across them without meaning to. A *Sunday Times* article from January 2020 – illustrated, of course, with an image from *Fifty Shades* – quotes a young student who reports that she started seeing strangulation material on Tumblr from the age of fourteen:

> I'd inadvertently see a lot of pornographic material because accounts would use the hashtags of other popular TV shows or media to bring followers to their porn sites ... After my experiences with Tumblr, I felt that choking was normalised as a sexual behaviour. It's shown as an expression of passion and it's something that girls are kind of groomed into doing, but it's only recently that I see that being critiqued as something criminal.[38]

Porn platforms profit from a process of escalation, introducing users to milder content, and then – for those who are susceptible – suggesting more and more extreme and addictive content as the viewer is gradually desensitised. For many users, that desensitisation leads inexorably towards BDSM, and, once a taste for creative forms of violence and degradation has developed, it may not stay confined to solitary fantasy.

One convicted domestic abuser interviewed by Dr Scott Hampton gives the game away when he confesses that 'I never would have thought of [strangulation] until I saw it in a porno,' and the huge age skew in the survey data on sexual strangulation lends weight to his claim. Is it really plausible that all of these young people spontaneously decided that strangulation was, as Gigi Engle describes it, 'a very fun Sex act'? Or could the fact that this generation is the first to have been raised on online porn also be playing a role?

This is hard to prove for certain either way. There is no randomised double blind trial proving the link between porn use and sexual behaviour, and there never will be, says Clare McGlynn, professor of law at Durham University. But McGlynn draws a comparison with advertising: 'It's not that I watch adverts and then go out and buy a particular washing powder. But on some level it is having some influence on me, and companies spend billions on advertising.'[39] The comparison is a good one, but it also returns us to the troubling issue that I raised in the last chapter, because companies selling washing powder *are responding to demand*, and so, I'm sorry to say, are porn producers. Strangulation is a fashion spread by porn, but it is an elaboration on a theme that the porn industry did not create. That theme centres around violent men who are aroused by domination and insecure women who seek it out. It is the same theme we see in *Fifty Shades*, and sometimes in Mills & Boon novels. It isn't new, but it has been horribly exaggerated in the modern world.

And the liberal feminist appeal to consent isn't good enough. It cannot account for the ways in which the sexuality of impressionable young people can be warped by porn or other forms of cultural influence. It cannot convincingly explain why a woman who hurts *herself* should be understood as mentally ill, but a woman who asks *her partner* to hurt her is apparently exercising her sexual agency. Above all, the liberal feminist faith in consent relies on a fundamentally false premise: that who we are in the bedroom is different from who we are outside of it.

In a recent piece, the *Sunday Times* advice columnist Dolly Alderton repeated this foolish idea in her response to a letter by a 29-year-old woman concerned that she was repeatedly 'drawn to' misogynist men:

> I think everyone should be free to separate their sexuality from their politics, as long as every party has consented and is having

fun. What's important is that you don't confuse your crav-
ing for sexual objectification or domination with a need for a
misogynistic or dominating boyfriend . . . Put simply: you need
a kind, chill, respectful boyfriend in the streets and a filthy
pervert in the sheets. They do exist. I hope you have fun finding
one.[40]

Alderton's recommendation was that her respondent seek out
casual sex on dating apps with men who are willing to act
like dominating misogynists in the bedroom but who are also
'nice'. It's hard to think of a worse piece of advice. Liberal
feminists such as Alderton are not only telling young women
to meet up with strange men from the internet for sex, they are
also telling them to pre-select those men on the basis of their
desire for violence.

Any man who can maintain an erection while beating up his
partner is a man to steer well clear of, but those with an interest in masochism don't want to hear that kind of grim truth,
and those with an interest in sadism don't want to be forced to
repress their desires. So the palatable option for liberal feminism is to draw a bright line between a person's sexuality and
their politics and then appeal desperately to 'consent' in an
attempt to ride the tiger of male sexuality. The problem is that,
while masochistic women may want to *play at* being raped,
they do not want to *actually be raped*. And yet seeking out a
man who is turned on by violence may well result in exactly
this outcome.

When the musician Andy Anokye (also known as Solo 45)
was accused of assaulting a number of women – committing
acts that included strangling them, waterboarding them, and
holding a gun to one woman's head and a cloth soaked in
bleach to the face of another – he offered a simple explanation
for his behaviour: it turned him on. This twenty-first-century
Marquis de Sade told Bristol Crown Court in 2020 that he was
aroused by dacryphilia, a fetish for terrified sobbing, which had

motivated him to seek out victims to terrorise sexually. One victim told the court that Anokye's abuse had been so bad that at one point she had 'wanted to die'.[41]

Anokye's defence team claimed that the five women who gave evidence against him had all consented to the acts of violence he inflicted, but – thankfully – the jury were not convinced by this narrative. In March 2020, he was unanimously convicted of twenty-one rapes, five counts of false imprisonment, two counts of assault by penetration, and two of assault occasioning actual bodily harm. He will serve at least twenty-four years in prison.[42]

During their investigation, detectives used video recovered from Anokye's phone to track down other women who had been subjected to his violence. Several of these women gave evidence for the prosecution, but one did not. Detectives described the videos featuring this woman as 'violent' and 'brutal', but she rejected that characterisation, telling the court, as a witness for the defence, 'it wasn't a rape – I consented to this behaviour and the activity.'[43]

Let's pretend for a moment that every one of Anokye's victims had responded to his violence just as this woman responded to it. She experienced exactly the same kind of abuse as the other women, but, for whatever reason, she didn't object to it. Liberal feminists would have us believe that if, by chance, all of his victims had felt this way, then Anokye would have done nothing wrong. His actions would no longer be shocking, misogynist and criminal. They might even be considered revolutionary, just like Sade's ('Do Whatever You Desire' read the placard at the 1968 student protest that Sade's biographer, Gonzague Saint Bris, so admired – a piece of advice that Anokye followed to the letter).

This cannot hold. Either Anokye is a villain, or he isn't – his villainy can't be dependent on whether or not he was lucky in his choice of victim and happened to choose a woman who wouldn't complain when strangled, waterboarded and suffocated with bleach. The liberal feminist analysis of sexual violence is not only wrong but dangerous. It tells people – mostly men – that, if they discover in themselves a desire to hurt other people, they shouldn't resist it but should instead cultivate it, locking themselves into a cycle of positive reinforcement in which arousal in response to violence is rewarded by orgasm.

And it tells people – mostly women – with masochistic impulses that these desires, too, should be encouraged. That instead of running in terror from men with a taste for violence – as Rose Keller ran from Sade through the streets of Paris – women should instead stay and feed this taste, giving the sadist exactly what he wants, until one day his desires are no longer confined to the bedroom, and he no longer stops at 'no'.

7

People Are Not Products

Wherever armies are to be found, brothels are to be found also, and often with more or less explicit sanction from military authorities. For British Army officials in the 1880s, for instance, the necessary link between prostitution and the colonial project was simply common sense. The vast numbers of British men stationed in India needed to be provided with prostitutes, and the authorities would rather not have an epidemic of venereal disease on their hands. Thus there was a procurement system put in place. A circular memorandum from the quartermaster general, dated 1886, decreed that 'it is necessary to have a sufficient number of women [and] to take care that they are sufficiently attractive.'[1]

To acquire these women – described in this same memorandum as 'convenient arrangements' – British officials would typically show up in Indian villages and flourish a government order for prostitutes. 'The poor people are afraid to refuse or resist; their daughters are delivered up,'[2] reported one medical officer. These young women – many of them below the age of consent in Britain at the time – were bought for 3 rupees apiece and then kept effectively imprisoned in the army brothels.

The madams took their clothes away on arrival, leaving them with only a translucent gown that would be conspicuously scanty if they ever ventured out on the streets, making escape difficult. The girls were also controlled through economic coercion, since they were required to pay a daily fee for their lodging, and this fee was made deliberately higher than the tiny sums they were paid by punters, meaning that a prostitute accumulated debt the longer she 'worked', tying her to the brothel forever.[3]

We know these details about the misery of these long-dead women only because of the efforts of Josephine Butler, an English campaigner whom we might now describe as a 'feminist', although the word was not in use at the time. Butler did not accept the male need for 'convenient arrangements'. To her mind, these Indian prostitutes were 'the women of a conquered race oppressed by their conquerors',[4] and she worked alongside other campaigners to successfully end the British Army's practice of institutionalised sexual slavery.

Butler is not remembered kindly by most twenty-first-century liberal feminists. Alison Phipps, professor of gender studies at the University of Sussex, describes Butler's movement in a paragraph dense with scare quotes:

> Today's reactionary feminists are descendants of nineteenth-century 'vice-fighters', Christian moralists and anti-miscegenationists, the bourgeois women enlisted by Fordism to 'improve' the working class, and those who ran the reformatories for 'wayward' Black girls and who abused them 'for their own good'. And the lineage is not just ideological. The Magdalene Laundries in Ireland, built in the eighteenth century to house 'fallen women', have more recently become Ruhama, an outreach organisation for women in prostitution. Anti-trafficking campaigns were prefigured by the 'white slavery' panics associated with nineteenth-century temperance.[5]

To 'wayward', 'improve', 'vice-fighters', 'fallen women' and 'white slavery' we might also add terms such as 'rescue', 'virtuous' and 'a life of sin' – all vocabulary used by nineteenth-century campaigners, and all now rejected by a new generation of feminists who regard prostitution very differently, and who are not only appalled by the abuses committed by some Victorians but are also allergic to their entire worldview.

In particular, the religious inflection of Victorian moralising is anathema to a determinedly secular contemporary feminist movement. Josephine Butler was a Christian, and her faith was the key driving force in her work. And although she was both a slavery abolitionist and an early supporter of women's suffrage – two issues that place her on 'the right side of history' from the vantage point of today – she is also condemned on other counts. One historian, for instance, describes Butler's campaign against the army brothels as dependent on an 'image of a helpless Indian womanhood' and describes Butler as a collaborator 'in the ideological work of empire'.[6] You'd never guess, reading her modern critics, that Butler's goal was to stop British men raping Indian girls.

I refuse to condemn Butler or to put sneering scare quotes around the terminology that she and her allies used to describe their work. Yes, she used the Bible in her attempts to help women out of prostitution, quoting from the gospels as she sat on the floor and picked oakum with people confined to English workhouses. And, no, she didn't manage to tear down the British Empire, or even to stray far outside of the imperialist paradigm. But then she also took destitute women and girls into her home and nursed them as they died from venereal disease contracted through prostitution, and how many twenty-first-century feminists can boast of similar deeds?

If we are to understand the workings of the sex trade within their historical context, we should look to Josephine Butler before we look to her modern critics, because to succumb to chronological snobbery in this case is to commit a fatal error.

Prostitution has never been a matter of personal choice or female empowerment. Rather, the role of 'buyer' versus 'seller' has always been determined not only by sex but also by race, nationality and – above all – class.

An ancient solution

Earlier in this book, I laid out the ways in which average male and female sexuality differ, and I made the case for this difference being a product of evolution rather than merely culture. One of the most important differences between the sexes is that men are higher in the quality that psychologists call 'sociosexuality' – the desire for sexual variety. This means that, on average, men are much more likely than women to desire casual sex.

This sexuality gap produces a mismatch between male and female desire at the population level. There are a lot more straight men than there are straight women looking for casual sex, meaning that many of these men are left frustrated by the lack of willing casual partners. As we have seen, in the post-sexual revolution era, the solution to this mismatch has often been to encourage women (ideally young, attractive ones) to overcome their reticence and have sex 'like a man', imitating male sexuality en masse. The thesis of this book is that this solution has been falsely presented as a form of sexual liberation for women, when in fact it is nothing of the sort, since it serves male, not female, interests. But one of the points I have been keen to stress throughout is that, although our current sexual culture has significant problems, this does not mean that the sexual cultures of the past were idyllic. All societies must find some kind of solution to the sexuality gap, and those solutions can be anti-woman in many diverse ways.

Our modern solution is to encourage *all* women, from every class, to meet the male demand for casual sex. In contrast, the solution adopted by most societies in the period before the invention of reliable contraception was for *the majority* of women to have sex only within marriage (whether that be monogamous or polygynous), while *a minority* of poor women were tasked with absorbing all that excess male sexual desire. Aside from a handful of high-class courtesans and call girls who might attain some degree of social status – usually having come from poor backgrounds originally – the prostituted class has historically been composed of women with no other options: the destitute, those abandoned by their partners, those addicted to drugs or alcohol, and those captured in warfare or tricked by traffickers. Prostitution is an ancient solution to the sexuality gap, and it is not a pleasant one.

It's very difficult to explain the wretchedness of the prostituted class if you believe the modern liberal feminist claims about the sex industry. Why would women be so profoundly averse to selling sex if it were not really any different from selling some other product or service? And why would Indian families want either to 'refuse or resist' when British Army officials came for their daughters?

Liberal feminists attempt to explain this phenomenon as a result of stigma. They point out that prostitution is stigmatised, which is true, and they argue that stigmatisation makes life difficult and dangerous for prostitutes, which is also true, but they don't explain why the stigma would arise in the first place, except to suggest, as does the sex-positive historian Kate Lister, that 'cultures that repressed sexuality' are to blame, because, 'as patriarchal, puritanical attitudes towards sex developed in the West, women's sexuality came in for particular censure.'[7]

Some liberal feminists go even further. One 2014 academic paper, for instance, titled 'Sex work undresses patriarchy with every trick!' argues that: 'It is precisely because sex work constantly challenges patriarchy, stereotypes and the normative understanding of feminine sexuality that it evokes a sense of unease and agitation amongst those seeking to bear the torch of patriarchy.'[8] But 'patriarchy' (if by this we mean a social system that prioritises male interests over female ones) does not necessarily demand the censure of female sexuality at all, at least not consistently. Men might not want *their* wives or daughters to have illicit sex, but they are often quite happy for the wives and daughters of *other* men to do so. Which means that reserving a prostituted class for the purposes of male enjoyment suits male interests very nicely. Why, then, would 'patriarchal, puritanical' ideology explain the intense and cross-cultural reluctance that women almost always feel when faced with the prospect of becoming a member of this class?

There is a much more convincing explanation for the deeply visceral aversion that women typically feel in relation to prostitution. As I laid out in chapter 2, our evolutionary history has led to men and women pursuing different reproductive strategies as a consequence of their different reproductive roles. As the evolutionary biologist David Buss writes:

> From the moment of conception, when the one tiny sperm joins the nutrient-rich egg, women are already contributing much more than the man. The asymmetry in investment does not end there. It is the woman who incubates the fertilised egg within her body. It is the woman who transfers calories from her body through the placenta to the developing embryo ... It is the woman who bears the burden of nine full months of pregnancy, an astonishingly long investment compared to most mammals.[9]

Given all this, is it any surprise that women are picky about who they have sex with? In a world without reliable contraception, the decision to have sex is far more consequential for a woman than it is for a man, since the possibility of an unwanted pregnancy leaves her with some very stark options: raising a baby without support from a mate, an attempted abortion, or infanticide. In our species' history, women have never had the option to rip and run.

The Pill has existed for seventy years, while *Homo sapiens* has existed for approximately 200,000 years. We evolved in an environment in which sex led to pregnancy, and these psychological adaptations remain with us. Of course nature *can* be overcome, to an extent – we all live modern lives that are very different from those of our ancient ancestors – but it is very hard to remove deeply embedded adaptations from the human mind.

Emotionally, if not legally, it is difficult to distinguish prostitution from rape. The feminist campaigner Rachel Moran, who was in prostitution from the age of fifteen through to twenty-two, describes her own emotional response as identical to that experienced during sexual abuse:

> I felt the same sickening nausea and rising panic that is inherent to conventional sexual abuse in each prostitution experience I ever had, and I felt that regardless of whether or not a man stayed within the agreed sexual boundaries. ... When we understand that the sex paid for in prostitution shares so many of its characteristics with the sex stolen in rape, it makes sense that so many prostituted women make clear parallels between the two experiences.[10]

The whole point of paid sex is that it must be paid for. It is not mutually desired by both parties – one party is there unwillingly, in exchange for money, or sometimes other goods such as drugs, food or shelter. The person being paid must ignore her own lack of sexual desire, or even her bone-deep revulsion. She must suppress her most self-protective instincts in the service of another person's sexual pleasure. This is why the sex industry typically attracts only the poorest and the most desperate women – these are the people who don't have the means to resist it.

Prostitution denies women what they are evolved to want: the opportunity to choose their mates. Instead, prostitutes are forced to have unwanted sex with men that they do not find even remotely attractive. And, in the era before reliable contraception, unwanted pregnancy was often the result, as is evident from archeological evidence such as that found in an excavation in Buckinghamshire, England, which uncovered ninety-seven infant skeletons buried under a Roman brothel.[11] Even in the modern world, in low- and middle-income countries, where access to contraception can be unreliable, female prostitutes have about a one in four chance of being impregnated by a client in any given year.[12] Sex may be meaningless fun for the clients, but it is neither fun nor meaningless for the women, or for the children they bear.

$20 and $200

There is a strange thing that happens in the political discourse on the sex industry. Usually, people who identify with the liberal left are concerned with championing the interests of the most economically marginalised people – the poor over the rich, the worker over the boss, and so on. But when it comes to prostitution, that position is slyly reversed. Rather than talking about the women at the bottom of the industry – the very poor, drug addicted or trafficked – it is more common to see liberal feminists drawing attention to those in the most elite slice of the industry. It is the highest earning, rather than the lowest earning, who find themselves with the most vigorous allies on the left.

I don't dispute that there are some self-described sex workers who are not in poverty and who, moreover, not only support the decriminalisation of prostitution on empirical grounds but also insist that sex work is just like any other kind of work. These women are particularly prominent in the media and on platforms such as Twitter. Compared with other women in prostitution, they are disproportionately likely to be white, Western and university educated. Furthermore, by definition, those speaking freely and publicly about their experiences in the industry are not being tightly pimped, are fluent in English, and have access to the internet. They are representative only of the most comparatively fortunate end of the sex-work spectrum.

In contrast, the women who campaign for the so-called Nordic model, which criminalises buyers and pimps but decriminalises sellers, tend to have different biographies. They are much more likely to have left the sex industry before beginning campaigning work and to have been in brothel- and street-based prostitution rather than escorting or camming. They are also much more likely to have been born in poverty.

This is an observation that many advocates of decriminalisation find annoying. Juno Mac and Molly Smith, for instance, the authors of *Revolting Prostitutes: The Fight for Sex Workers' Rights*, describe the bind in which they find themselves, with their views as sex workers instantly discredited because of their class backgrounds: 'Many sex worker activists find that their testimonies are dismissed in feminist spaces on the grounds that, by virtue of being activists, they are not representative; that they speak from an exceptional, privileged and anomalous perspective.'[13]

Mac and Smith both have PhDs, but, even without knowing this information about their biographies, their middle-class accents would give them away. As would mine, of course – as a columnist and author, I am speaking from a platform to which the vast majority of people simply do not have access. By definition, this is a public discussion to which only the relatively privileged can contribute.

But it is important to pay attention to the class backgrounds of activist sex workers, not as a 'gotcha' to shut down discussion, but because one's economic interests have a profound effect on one's personal preferences. Once you start paying attention, you notice how many of these activists have had an unusual experience of the sex industry. Julie Bindel, the investigative journalist and campaigner against sexual violence, writes of some of the most prominent voices in media discussions of the sex industry:

> Many of those high-profile pro-prostitution lobbyists who speak as 'sex workers' are what I would call 'tourists'. Melissa Gira-Grant for example, who is highly educated and earning her living as a journalist; Brooke Magnanti, who holds a PhD, has written several books, and works as a scientist; and Douglas Fox, whose partner owns one of the largest escort agencies in Britain, are not representative of the sex trade.[14]

This sleight of hand is partly enabled by the fact that the term 'sex worker' has such a loose meaning. Sometimes it might refer – as in Magnanti's case – to what is sometimes called 'full contact' sex work. Others – such as Gira-Grant – may have only ever done cam work. Most egregiously, a man such as Douglas Fox is also able to describe himself as an 'independent male sex worker' and can even retain a prominent position in the International Union of Sex Workers, despite the fact that he is actually a pimp.[15]

Within the academy, it is particularly common to see researchers describe themselves as 'sex workers' while being deliberately vague about the exact nature of their involvement in the industry. When the phrases 'listen to sex workers' and 'speaking as a sex worker' carry such a premium, it's unsurprising to see such claims bandied around by people who might be better described as (to use Bindel's phrase) 'tourists'.

This is a longstanding issue in the sex workers' rights movement. One of the first and most influential organisations advocating for the full decriminalisation of prostitution was COYOTE (Call Off Your Old Tired Ethics), founded in San

Francisco in 1973 and often described in the media as 'the first prostitutes' union'.[16] But when the sociologist Elizabeth Bernstein conducted eighteen months of fieldwork among prostitutes in San Francisco, she found the COYOTE membership to be highly unrepresentative:

> The vast majority of COYOTE's members are white, middle-class and well-educated, just as their political opponents claim. They are predominantly call-girls, escorts, exotic dancers and masseuses; a few are fetish specialists, such as dominatrixes or 'switches' (who alternate between domination and submission). Many work out of expensively-furnished homes or rented 'work spaces' by placing advertisements in newspapers, earning enough money not only to cover expenses, but also to help finance alternative artistic and intellectual careers . . . The average hourly fee, whether or not one is 'in business for herself,' is $200.

Bernstein described COYOTE's monthly meetings, in which:

> New members often introduce themselves by telling their 'coming out' stories ('I graduated from Smith College with a BA in philosophy, then I moved here to become a sex-worker') and are met with hearty applause. Being a sex-worker is about taking pleasure in sex, unleashing repressed energies, or exploring the socially-deemed dangerous border zones of eroticism.

This is in contrast to the prostitutes Bernstein described as being at 'the other end of the continuum': homeless women, addicted to crack or heroin, who would sell sex for $20 and then immediately spend the proceeds on drugs. Most of these women were tightly controlled by pimps and were visibly sickly and distressed.[17]

Elizabeth Bernstein is a long way from being a sex trade abolitionist, and I imagine she would strongly disagree with much of what I have to say in this book.[18] Nevertheless, she draws attention to a problem with the discourse on the sex industry that typically goes unacknowledged. The directive 'listen to sex workers' is commonly used by the decriminalisation lobby, but *which ones*?

Luxury beliefs

The psychologist Rob Henderson has coined the term 'luxury beliefs' to describe the kind of ideas and opinions that confer status on the rich at very little cost while taking a toll on the poor.[19] These are, he theorises, a form of Veblen good, named for the sociologist Thorstein Veblen – that is, products that do not obey the usual rules of supply and demand but instead are desired by consumers *because* they are expensive, rather than in spite of this fact. But as luxury consumables have become easier to manufacture and thus more affordable, the rich have had to cast around for new Veblen goods. Therefore, writes Henderson:

> The affluent have decoupled social status from goods, and re-attached it to beliefs ... The logic is akin to conspicuous consumption – if you're a student who has a large subsidy from your parents and I do not, you can afford to waste $900 and I can't, so wearing a Canada Goose jacket is a good way of advertising your superior wealth and status. Proposing policies that will cost you as a member of the upper class less than they would cost me serve the same function.

In the elite circles of the media, NGOs and top universities, repeating a phrase such as 'sex work is work' confers status on the speaker. It suggests an admirable open-mindedness, a rebellious attitude towards bourgeois sexual norms, and an empathetic relationship with the imagined figure of 'the sex worker' – that is, an independent entrepreneur who doesn't mind the sex itself but does mind the intrusion of the state into her business. Proponents of this luxury belief may share hashtags on Twitter such as #supportsexworkers and #decrimnow, and they will tell anyone who disagrees with them to 'listen to sex workers', but they will typically never have met or spoken with anyone who has experienced $20 prostitution, or perhaps even $200 prostitution. But since the term 'sex worker' collapses the two categories together, the class distinctions can be easily obscured.

But that doesn't mean that the class distinctions go away. Support for the decriminalisation and normalisation of prostitution may not obviously *look* like a luxury belief, since proponents will typically use the vocabulary of oppression and marginalisation. But in effect *it is* a luxury belief, since the costs are not borne by the upper classes who gain status by expressing support for such a policy but instead by the lower class people – overwhelmingly women – who are most likely to actually end up in the sex industry.

Decriminalisation or legalisation of the sex industry increases the demand for commercial sex. In countries that have adopted these legal models, the proportion of the male population who have ever bought sex is higher, and the sex tourism industry is larger. Given that the number of women who will willingly enter the sex trade is very small, when demand grows, unwilling women must be sought out in order to meet it.

In the global sex industry, it is poor countries that provide the 'product' and rich countries that provide the demand. The brothels of the UK, Netherlands and Germany are filled with women from poor parts of the European Union, in particular Romania, as well as women from West Africa and Southeast Asia,[20] some of whom have been forcibly trafficked, while the rest are there as a result of varying degrees of poverty. Meanwhile, the brothels of Bangkok that cater for tourists are filled with sex buyers from Europe, Australia and North America. The buyers tend to have lighter coloured skins than the sellers because sex is sold in only one direction along the economic gradient.

Walk through Patpong, one of Bangkok's most popular red-light districts, and you will see a lot of white men. The same was true during the Vietnam War, when Bangkok was one of the preferred destinations for American soldiers' week of 'R&R': officially, 'Rest & Recuperation', unofficially, 'Rape & Run.'[21] The historian Meredith Lair describes the American military's implicit sanction of prostitution during the war:

> At euphemistic massage parlors and steam baths all over South Vietnam, soldiers could get fellatio or intercourse for as little as $2. Military authorities dismissed brothels on American bases with a nod and a wink, providing medical care to prostitutes and Johns alike, which sent a strong signal to American soldiers that their exploitation of Vietnamese women was not only excused but also sanctioned as a bonus for a year's worth of service.[22]

Sex tourism destinations still cluster around US military bases. In Korea, thousands of women – including 5,000 Filipinas and even more Russians – are located around the bases, and there is pressure to 'import' younger and younger women from more 'exotic' backgrounds to meet the demand for variety.[23] The British Army officials in the 1880s who procured young Indian women for their soldiers were conforming to an historical norm.

Many sex buyers are deeply and profoundly racist and make no effort to conceal this fact, speaking openly and in crude terms about their contempt for the women from whom they buy sex. Both in online reviews and in interviews with researchers, race is featured prominently in buyers' assessments of the 'product', and it is not uncommon to come across nasty pieces of racist slang – LBFM ('little brown fucking machines') is, for instance, used to refer to Southeast Asian women. 'I made a list in my mind,' reports one London sex buyer. 'I told myself that I'll be with different races, e.g. Japanese, Indian, Chinese . . . Once I have been with them I tick them off the list. It's like a shopping list.'[24]

Some advocates of decriminalisation or legalisation are sanguine about this racialised dynamic, pointing out that there are plenty of other industries in which migrant workers predominate. And although they do recognise that selling sex is risky – with a homicide rate many times higher for prostituted women than for non-prostituted,[25] as well as a shockingly high all-cause mortality rate due to drug and alcohol related deaths[26] – they point out that it is not the only line of work that comes with danger. Brooke Magnanti, for instance, a former escort who writes under the pen name Belle de Jour, compares a career selling sex to a career as a deep-sea fisherman – both dangerous options, yes, but both legitimate forms of work.[27]

When this idea is taken to its logical conclusion, we end up with the sterile language of business introduced to the brothel or the alleyway. In academic writing that attempts to impose this framework, pimps and madams engage in 'sex work management',[28] rape becomes a 'contract breach',[29] and violence, pregnancy and disease become 'occupational health risks'.[30] The horror of what is actually happening is deliberately obscured, because we're not supposed to feel horror. The cerebral, liberal thing to do is to resist such emotional impulses and regard prostitution as much the same as deep-sea fishing, only with an added layer of pointless stigma – a relic from less enlightened times.

The redistribution of sex

Throughout this book, I've used the term 'sexual disenchantment' to describe both an historical process and a political claim. I've borrowed the term from Aaron Sibarium, who writes:

> Where past sexual regimes constrained who could have sex with whom, and for what ends, today's attacks such constraints as benighted and domineering – promising, like classical liberalism, to let individuals do as they please. A marriage, a one-night stand, a 'throuple,' a hook-up, a brothel: these are all equally valid means of getting sex, which has no inherent value beyond what consenting adults assign to it. If the scientific revolution disenchanted the world, *a la* Weber, the sexual revolution disenchanted sex in the process of deregulating it.[31]

Liberal feminism incorporates sexual disenchantment as an article of faith, insisting that it is *a good thing* that sex is now regarded as without inherent value in the post-sexual revolution era. But, in practice, liberal feminist women do not generally behave as if they believe in the truth of sexual disenchantment. Almost no one does.

Sexual disenchantment is often appealed to by those who support the legalisation or decriminalisation of prostitution. It is common to hear proponents of this view compare sex work to other forms of work and challenge their critics to name the difference. This rhetorical move is effective only because it relies on a collective effort to believe in sexual disenchantment. If you want to be a good liberal, then you're not supposed to believe that sex has some kind of specialness to it that makes it different from other acts.

But even the best liberals do still *feel* that sex is somehow different, even if they struggle to articulate the difference. People care if their partner has sex with someone else, and not only because doing so involves breaking a promise. A quick browse of any online polyamorist forum will uncover a lot of people who are trying very hard to practise 'ethical non-monogamy' and yet are tormented by sexual jealousy.

And people know intuitively that a boss asking for a blow job in exchange for a promotion is entirely different from a boss asking for overtime in exchange for a promotion. I find it perplexing that so many liberal feminists who argue vigorously that 'sex work is work' are hyper-sensitive to any suggestion of sexual impropriety in their own workplaces. These women recoil at being asked out for dinner by a male colleague or being touched casually on an arm or leg, describing such acts as 'sexual harassment'. But if *that* is sexual harassment, then how should we describe what goes on in a brothel?

Cynically, I suspect that the different attitude towards these two kinds of workplace comes down to self-interest. I don't mean to suggest that middle- and upper-class women don't suffer from the costs of the sexual revolution, because of course they do. Hook-up culture also has a pernicious effect on Ivy League and Russell Group campuses, and the boyfriends of economically privileged women are just as likely to be addled by porn as any other men.

But there are certain forms of sexual harm that are far more threatening to people who are simultaneously young, female *and poor*. Prostitution is one of them. And it is telling that, when the terrible consequences of sexual disenchantment are likely to personally affect women who are not otherwise at risk of ending up in prostitution, the inconsistency is laid bare.

For instance, in recent years there has been much media outrage in response to instances of landlords offering young would-be tenants 'sex for rent' arrangements. Liberal publications such as *Glamour* magazine describe such offers as 'sickening' and 'terrifying',[32] while *The Guardian* bemoans the fact that 'more is not being done' to prosecute landlords who post such ads.[33] The Labour Party has promised to act on the issue if returned to government by introducing a specific offence in relation to offering 'sex in lieu of rent',[34] and the Liberal Democrats support this call for a new law.[35]

A spokesperson for Rape Crisis England & Wales points out that 'agreeing to have sex with someone under the pressure and fear of homelessness, or in exchange for the basic right to have somewhere to live, does not equate to agreeing by choice . . . Any sexual activity without consent is a very serious sexual offence.'[36] And yet this is a feminist organisation that states on its website that 'just because you are or have been involved in the sex industry, does not mean that you have experienced sexual violence'[37] – in other words, selling sex for money can be done with consent, but selling sex for rent cannot. And while Labour and the Liberal Democrats are apparently appalled at the 'sex for rent' phenomenon, the latter are officially in favour of decriminalising the sale of sex for cash,[38] and the previous leader of the former – Jeremy Corbyn – has stated that he considers the decriminalisation of the sex industry to be the 'more civilised' option.[39]

Why should exchanging sex directly for money be decriminalised and destigmatised, whereas exchanging sex for accommodation should not? We are all quite happy to recognise that rent has a cash value when it comes, for instance, to negotiating nanny contracts. Forgive me for being cynical, but could it be because we are in the midst of a housing crisis, which means that middle-class young women – the daughters of politicians and journalists – are newly anxious about their ability to pay rent? With that anxiety made more acute by media coverage that often highlights the particular vulnerability of students to 'sex for rent' proposals, with 'sordid offers [found] across university cities, including Oxford, Bristol and Brighton' – cities home to some of the most prestigious universities in the UK.[40]

Or take, as another example of liberal feminist inconsistency, the panic around incels: involuntarily celibate men who gather online to complain about their lack of success in attracting girlfriends. In 2018, the libertarian economist Robin Hanson wrote a blog post in which he voiced sympathy for incels:

> One might plausibly argue that those with much less access to sex suffer to a similar degree as those with low income, and might similarly hope to gain from organising around this identity, to lobby for redistribution along this axis and to at least implicitly threaten violence if their demands are not met . . . Sex could be directly redistributed, or cash might be redistributed in compensation.[41]

All hell broke loose on progressive media. *Slate* asked if Hanson was 'America's Creepiest Economist'[42] and Moira Donegan in *Cosmopolitan* expressed outrage:

> Central to the incel ideology is the idea that sex with another person – specifically, penetrative sex with women – isn't a privilege for men, but a right. Incels talk about sex with 'Stacys,' their term for attractive women, the way that more reasonable people talk about food, water, and shelter: as a basic necessity for survival . . . Women are not interchangeable, we are not commodities.[43]

Obviously I agree. I don't think that incels are owed sexual access to anyone, whether or not 'cash is redistributed in compensation'. But note the difference in tone between a passage such as this – '*we* don't owe you sex' and '*our* vaginas' – compared to other progressive pieces on sex work, including those written by Donegan or published in *Slate* and *Cosmopolitan*. When it is the sexual integrity of prostituted women that's at stake, a ruthless pragmatism takes hold, and liberal feminists are concerned only with reducing the harm resulting from stigma. But when it is non-prostituted women whose bodies are at risk of 'redistribution', suddenly sexual disenchantment is forgotten, to be replaced by pure rage. *How dare* incels think that beautiful women would even give them the time of day?

This is the rage that comes from knowing, deep down, that sex *is* different from other forms of social interaction, which also means that selling sex is inherently different from any other kind of act. Vednita Carter, prostitution survivor and anti-sex trafficking activist, puts the point succinctly: 'People ask me "what is the inherent harm of prostitution?" – the inherent harm is the sex act itself.'[44]

Cultural death grip syndrome

'Death grip syndrome' is a quasi-medical term used to describe the impotence that can result from excessive porn use. It's partly a physical problem caused by aggressive masturbation leading to desensitisation, but it's also partly a psychological problem caused by an overload of sexual stimuli. Sufferers of death grip syndrome – almost all of them men – become incapable of having sex with a real person because their responses have been gradually deadened.

In chapter 5 I wrote about the fact that porn seems to have a paradoxical effect on users, incentivising them to have *less* sex with real people while simultaneously exposing them to *more* intense sexual stimuli. That paradoxical effect does not confine itself to the privacy of the user's bedroom. As public life has become ever more hyper-sexualised, I propose that we have entered an era of cultural death grip syndrome. We are now routinely exposed to so much sexual stimuli in the course of daily life that it no longer has much effect on us.

When Wonderbra released their famous 'Hello Boys' ad campaign, featuring Eva Herzigová admiring her own boosted cleavage, the posters were so distracting to motorists that they reportedly caused car crashes. That was in 1994. In contrast, try walking down any British high street today and keep a tally of how many lingerie-clad boobs and bums you see within a ten-minute interval: in shop windows, on the sides of buses, and on the covers of newspapers and magazines.

My local shopping centre currently has on display a six-foot-high photo of a model in a swimsuit licking the inside of another model's open mouth. This is far raunchier than the 1994 'Hello Boys' photo, but I would never usually have noticed it, since such images are so common now that they are little more than wallpaper. In a free market, with no moralising impediment, sexualisation will go in one direction, and one direction only, and for a simple reason: sex sells, and businesses know it.

Occasionally, a new cultural event will push at the boundaries of propriety with enough alacrity to attract attention. Most recently, the music video for the song 'WAP' ('Wet Ass Pussy'), by the American rappers Cardi B and Megan Thee Stallion, was praised by liberal commentators, who interpreted the pornified aesthetic and explicit lyrics as, in the words of one *Guardian* columnist, 'an unabashed celebration of female sexuality'.[45]

But this was a strange kind of celebration. Even if we assume that the repeated use of the word 'whore' in the lyrics is to be taken figuratively, there is plenty else in the track to suggest a transactional attitude towards sex. The male object of lust described in the lyrics is assessed according to two standards: the size of his 'king cobra' and the size of his bank balance. 'Pay my tuition', pleads Megan to this imagined man, who must 'make it rain' if he wants her sexual favours. 'Ask for a car' during sex, 'spit on his mic' to secure a record deal, 'let me tell you how I got this ring' – the sexual generosity described is all in service not of female pleasure but of material gain.

'WAP' has very little to do with authentic female sexuality, but it does provide a very revealing insight into the worst side of *male* sexuality – specifically, a compulsive and dehumanising side of male sexuality that is readily exploited by those in search of profit. Because, while there are almost no women who really believe in the idea of sexual disenchantment, even if they pretend otherwise, there is a minority of men who do believe in it, at least up to a point. They care about youth, and they care about looks, but otherwise they don't care who they're ejaculating into, and they certainly don't care if that person is enjoying themselves. If given the chance, these men will treat their sexual partners as unfeeling orifices. Remember the memorandum from the quartermaster general in 1886, quoted at the beginning of this chapter: 'it is necessary to have a sufficient number of women [and] to take care that they are sufficiently attractive.'[46] That is the punter's view of the matter.

This is a form of male sexuality that many women do not understand, since it is so different from typical female sexuality. But anyone who questions its existence should take a look at the comments that men leave on sites such as Punternet which are dedicated to customer reviews of prostitutes. A project put together by a group of Canadian feminists called 'The Invisible Men' (since replicated in other countries) collects quotes from these sites to demonstrate how little regard punters have for the people to whom they buy sexual access.[47] It doesn't make for nice reading.

Cultural pornification puts the logic of these men at the helm. It takes a – frankly – psychopathic view of human sexuality and allows it to leach out into public life. It treats people as fungible – that is, replaceable and interchangeable: in sexual terms, merely a collection of relevant body parts. A tongue that could belong to anyone licking the inside of a mouth that could belong to anyone. It is sex stripped down to its barest mechanics.

'Thanks to OnlyFans'

Only a culture in thrall to the worst of male sexuality could have eroticised the dick pic and its amputated female counterparts. I don't know what men think we are supposed to do with their dick pics, but I know of no woman who would masturbate to an image in which the rest of the person has been cropped away, leaving only a slab of flesh ready to be laid out on the anatomist's table. Typical female sexuality isn't orientated towards these kinds of images. But the internet abounds with them.

Many young women on social media have progressed smoothly from posting selfies – the subject of much media discussion only a decade ago – to posting 'belfies' (butt selfies). Instagram and TikTok, in particular, are filled with the youthful breasts and buttocks of women desperate for some positive male attention. For some of these women, posting sexualised images of themselves online can set them on a path towards setting up an account on OnlyFans, a platform that allows 'creators' (overwhelmingly women) to earn money by giving 'users' (overwhelmingly men) subscription access to online content, most of which is pornographic. If you are already used to marketing sexy photos of yourself for 'likes', marketing those photos for actual money may not seem like an especially consequential step.

And the incentives are attractive. Every now and again, a tweet by a previously unknown OnlyFans creator will go viral, as she (always she) shares photos of the house she has been able to buy 'thanks to OnlyFans'. But, as the blogger Thomas Hollands has found in his detailed analysis of the OnlyFans model, such rags-to-riches cases are very unusual.[48] The distribution of income on OnlyFans is highly unequal, with the top 1 per cent of creators making 33 per cent of all the money. Using the Gini index – a standard measure of economic inequality – Hollands finds OnlyFans to be significantly more unequal than South Africa, the most unequal country in the world. The tiny minority of creators who do well on the site are mostly existing celebrities, meaning that the women who post 'thanks to OnlyFans' success stories on social media are not at all representative of ordinary creators but, rather, more like those rare customers who walk out of a casino millionaires, having put it all on red.

In fact, most of the women on OnlyFans probably make a loss, given the amount of time they must spend creating content and engaging with users. The median creator attracts only thirty subscribers, but she carries just as much risk of public exposure and harassment as her more successful counterparts. OnlyFans is not anything like as dangerous as street- or brothel-based prostitution – it's definitely more like $200 than $20 prostitution – but it does come with perils, primarily to a woman's long-term relationship prospects, which are key to her long-term happiness.

As I laid out in chapter 4, most men take a very negative attitude towards what they consider to be a history of promiscuity in a potential marriage partner, even if they don't necessarily admit to this publicly. This means that, although an OnlyFans account may provide a woman with a short-term injection of self-esteem, and perhaps also an injection of cash, it will also limit the pool of men who are willing to marry her, because OnlyFans is to the marriage market as a criminal record is to the jobs market.

And there are other costs associated with turning yourself into a sexual commodity. The supermodel Emily Ratajkowski, widely considered to be one of the most beautiful women in the world, writes in her autobiography *My Body* about the dysfunction that results from seeing oneself always through a commercialised lens. For instance, Ratajkowski insists on watching herself in the mirror when she has sex with her husband, 'so that I can see that I'm real.'[49] She's aware that this isn't healthy.

But, in an age of dating apps, it isn't only supermodels who end up with their sexuality warped by a sexual marketplace that turns people into products. Tinder and its rivals are not dissimilar from shopping sites. The format encourages users to browse the available merchandise and select their preferred options from the comfort of their homes, with very little effort and no intimacy whatsoever.

In a 2015 article on dating apps in *Vanity Fair*, one male user describes the voracious impulse that the apps encourage:

> 'Guys view everything as a competition,' he elaborates with his deep, reassuring voice. 'Who's slept with the best, hottest girls?' With these dating apps, he says, 'you're always sort of prowling. You could talk to two or three girls at a bar and pick the best one, or you can swipe a couple hundred people a day – the sample size is so much larger. It's setting up two or three Tinder dates a week and, chances are, sleeping with all of them, so you could rack up 100 girls you've slept with in a year.'

Another interviewee is explicit about his instinct towards sexual consumerism, comparing Tinder to an online food delivery service – 'but you're ordering a person.'[50] This is, by his reckoning, a good thing.

And yet, despite all this convenience, Tinder causes its users more unhappiness than almost any other app.[51] In a further iteration of cultural death grip syndrome, users report that dating apps manage to turn what should be an exciting experience into a dull and depressing one, because an overabundance of options does not increase the sexual thrill but instead kills it.

I don't need to tell readers that street- and brothel-based prostitution is dangerous and traumatic. If you're reading this book, it's unlikely that you need to be persuaded on that point. But I think I do need to warn against the consequences of sexual disenchantment that go beyond the obvious. This means that, on a personal level, we can't just refuse to participate in the sex industry and then pat ourselves on the back for a job well done. I've made it clear already that I don't think it's possible to use porn ethically, and of course I'd apply that same rule to prostitution. But refusing to view people as products goes further than that: it demands that we challenge the disenchanted idea of what sex ought to be.

The very many articles with such headlines as '8 very necessary sex tips from sex workers' and '5 insightful sex tips from a professional sex worker'[52] betray a view of sex that is becoming disturbingly prevalent. Sex workers can act as sources of sex advice only if we understand sex to be a skillset that must be learned and refined across different partners, with good sex a result not of intimacy but of good technique. In this framing, sex becomes something that one does *to* another person, not *with* another person. All of the emotion is drained away, leaving the logic of the punter triumphant.

We must resist that logic at all costs. If we try and pretend that sex has no special value that makes it different from other acts, then we end up in some very dark places. If sex isn't worthy of its own moral category, then nor is sexual harassment or rape. If we accept that sex is merely a service that can be freely bought and sold, then we have no arguments left to make against the incels who want to 'redistribute' it or the army officials who want to offer their troops 'convenient arrangements'. If we voice no objection to the principle of 'sex sells', then we can hardly complain when our public spaces are saturated with hyper-sexuality and we find ourselves scrolling through would-be sexual partners on a dating app in the same way we scroll through any other kind of consumable. Once you permit the idea that people can be products, everything is corroded.

8

Marriage Is Good

In making the case against the sexual revolution, I've often run across a particular kind of problem that is by no means unique to this subject. I call it the problem of normal distribution.

The normal distribution is also known as the bell curve because the graph it produces looks rather like a bell. It is a continuous probability distribution that is symmetrical around the mean – meaning, in essence, that most of the data points cluster around the middle and, the further a value is from the mean, the less likely it is to occur. The normal distribution is found again and again in the sciences. The sizes of snowflakes, lifetimes of lightbulbs, and milk production of cows are all normally distributed.[1] So are human physical traits such as height, shoe size and birth weight.

Social phenomena are a little more complicated, but, even so, the normal distribution is often a good approximation for what we see across human populations. Sociosexuality, for instance (an interest in sexual variety), is close to being normally distributed. Most people are close to average, and a minority of unusual people are found at one or other pole, meaning that there are some people who have no interest whatsoever in casual sex, and some people who are off-the-charts horny. Importantly, though – as I first laid out in chapter 2 – the bell curves for men and for women are somewhat different, with the male mean further towards the higher end of the sociosexuality spectrum. This means that there are a lot more super-horny men than super-horny women, and a lot more super-not-horny women than super-not-horny men.

The problem of normal distribution is this: when you impose some change on a population, different people will experience it differently. It is very, very difficult to design a policy that will home in on just one group of people at just one point on the graph, leaving the rest of the curve unchanged. And when it comes to a big historical event such as the sexual revolution – which nobody designed, or even fully foresaw – that imprecision is even more marked.

Marital satisfaction is (almost) normally distributed.[2] Most people report being quite happy in their marriages, with a minority who report being very happy and another minority who report being very unhappy.

It used to be exceptionally difficult for those very unhappy couples to divorce. Journalist Megan McArdle describes the process of acquiring a divorce in nineteenth-century America:

> It took years, was expensive, and required proving that your spouse had abandoned you for an extended period with no financial support; was (if male) not merely discreetly dallying but flagrantly carrying on; or was not just belting you one now and again when you got mouthy, but routinely pummelling you within an inch of your life.
>
> After you got divorced, you were a pariah in all but the largest cities. If you were a desperately wronged woman you might change your name, taking your maiden name as your first name and continuing to use your husband's last name to indicate that you expected to continue living as if you were married (i.e. chastely) and expect to have some limited intercourse with

your neighbors, though of course you would not be invited to events held in a church, or evening affairs.

Financially secure women generally (I am not making this up) moved to Europe; Edith Wharton, who moved to Paris when she got divorced, wrote moving stories about the way divorced women were shunned at home.[3]

If you sought a divorce during this period, it was almost certainly because you were at the very unhappy tail of the normal distribution, and thus – and I don't think this is a controversial statement – deserving of help and sympathy. That was certainly the attitude of the social reformers who began to campaign for the liberalisation of divorce laws in the years following the Second World War. From roughly the 1960s onwards, and across the Western world, it suddenly became much easier to get divorced, and people who had been legally trapped in hellish marriages were freed from them, which was a good thing. But then came the problem of normal distribution.

In reading the parliamentary debates on what would become the 1969 Divorce Reform Act – the key piece of liberalising legislation in the UK – it does not appear that the supporters of the Bill knew what was coming. They believed that their reforms would be an act of kindness towards the small number of people on the unhappy tail of the normal distribution, but that the rest of the curve would be left intact. 'This Bill does not open the door to easy divorce,' announced Lord Stow Hill, onetime Attorney General. 'That door is wide open now, under the existing law, and it would be hard to open it wider.'[4]

And yet open it did. In the decade following the Divorce Reform Act, the number of divorces trebled and then kept rising, peaking in the 1980s.[5] Since then there has been a slight decline in the divorce rate, not because of a genuine return to marital longevity but, rather, because you can't get divorced if you don't get married in the first place, and marriage rates are at an historic low.[6] In 1968, 8 per cent of children were born to parents who were not married; in 2019, it was almost half.[7] Today, there are just two marriages for every divorce in the UK each year.[8] The institution of marriage, as it once was, is now more or less dead.

In the United States it is deader still. There, almost half of marriages end in divorce,[9] and there is also a new and significant class divide. Before the 1970s, the vast majority of Americans got married and stayed married, regardless of family income. Now, of those Americans in the top-third income bracket, 64 per cent are in an intact marriage, meaning they have only married once and are still in their first marriage. In contrast, only 24 per cent of Americans in the lower-third income bracket are in an intact marriage.[10] A durable marriage is fast becoming a luxury of the upper classes.

Of course, some marriages should end, and in those cases the liberalisation of divorce laws was a blessing. Although married women are not at greater risk of domestic violence than unmarried women – the opposite, in fact[11] – it is obviously better when abused wives do not face serious legal obstacles in trying to leave their husbands. The extreme unhappy tail of the normal distribution really did need to get divorced, and, before the reforms of the mid-twentieth century, they often couldn't.

But the problem of normal distribution made it impossible for the reforms to laser in on these extreme cases. Most modern divorces are not a consequence of domestic abuse[12] – most involve a couple growing apart, falling out of love, and trying for a fresh start. But, in many of these cases, the promise of happier alternative relationships remains unfulfilled, particularly for women, who are more likely than men to remain permanently single following divorce.[13] What's more, between a third and a half of divorced people in the UK report in surveys that they regret their decision to divorce.[14] There is a lot of space between 'happy' and 'irreparably unhappy'. In the past, those people remained married; now they usually don't.

And, in a culture of high divorce rates, even those marriages that last risk being undermined. When marriage vows are no longer truly binding, couples seem to become less confident in their relationships. One study by the American economist Betsey Stevenson, for instance, found that marital investment declined in the wake of no-fault divorce laws, with newly-wed couples in states that passed no-fault divorce about 10 per cent less likely to support a spouse through college or graduate school and 6 per cent less likely to have a child together.[15]

When marriage became impermanent, the institution as a whole was changed, and with it much else. I doubt very much that any of the well-meaning reformers of the 1960s ever envisioned such an outcome. Their intention had been a noble one: to offer a way out for people stuck in wretched marriages and to lift the stigma from the then tiny minority unfortunate enough to have been through divorce. But the problem of normal distribution interceded. There was always a threshold of dysfunction above which a marriage was considered beyond saving, and reformers intended to nudge it only a little. But as the marginal divorce made the next one more likely, and the one after that more likely still, that threshold went hurtling downwards at great speed.

My money, my choice

Divorce reforms were not solely responsible for the death of marriage, of course. They formed part of a suite of factors, all of which can be traced back to several important material changes of the mid-twentieth century. Lawmakers loosened the limits on divorce because the institution of marriage was already starting to stumble. Their reforms acted as a final shove.

The most important of these material changes was the invention of the contraceptive pill, which presents a particularly clear example of the sometimes unpredictable consequences of a technology shock. It's odd, in retrospect, that the introduction of a new form of contraception led to an *increase* rather than a decrease in the number of births out of wedlock, and yet that's exactly what happened. This was because the Pill ended the taboo on pre-marital sex, while not actually providing complete protection from pregnancy. It still doesn't, even though it remains the most popular method of prescribed contraception in the UK and the US:[16] with perfect use, the combined contraceptive pill is 99 per cent effective, but with typical use it is 91 per cent effective, meaning that around nine in 100 women taking it will get pregnant in a year.[17] Across a population, that is a huge number of unwanted babies.

The decriminalisation of abortion across the Western world, which arrived shortly after the introduction of the Pill, provided a 'back-up' option in these cases of contraceptive failure. In the contemporary United States, about half of women who have abortions report that they were using contraception when they became pregnant,[18] and about a quarter of all pregnancies end in abortion. For a married woman who can cope with an 'oops' baby, the Pill is a good option. But, for everyone else, it doesn't actually deliver what it's supposed to. And yet it was effective enough to change social norms dramatically. The columnist Virginia Ironside reflected in later life on the effect on young British women of the introduction of the Pill and the decriminalisation of abortion:

> It often seemed more polite to sleep with a man than to chuck him out of your flat. True, we'd been brought up to say 'no' to sex, but the only reason for that was because we might get pregnant . . . But now, armed with the pill, and with every man knowing you were armed with the pill, pregnancy was no longer a reason to say 'no' to sex. And men exploited this mercilessly. Now, for them, 'no' always meant 'yes'.[19]

From the 1970s onwards, it became much less common for women to wait until marriage or engagement before having sex. And while, in theory, *the choice* to refuse pre-marital sex still existed, in practice it became a much harder option to stick with. In twenty-first-century America, unusually old virgins report being stigmatised by their peers, and they are less favoured as relationship partners.[20] The stigma is stronger for male virgins, but – perhaps for the first time historically – it clings to female virgins too.

The sexual revolution gave women the opportunity to make the choice not to wait until marriage because so many people believed that new contraceptive methods meant that extramarital sex no longer carried the risk of an unwanted pregnancy. Of course it still did, but the decriminalisation of abortion was there as a back-up, meaning that no man need ever again fear a shotgun wedding. When motherhood became a biological choice for women, fatherhood became a social choice for men. Or, as the comedian Dave Chappelle has put it (in jest, but describing a very real attitude): 'Not only do [women] have the right to choose, I don't believe they should have to consult anybody except for a physician. . . . Gentlemen, that is fair. But ladies, to be fair to us, if you decide to have the baby, the man should not have to pay . . . My money, my choice.'[21]

Plenty of modern men seem to agree with Chappelle's take. Before the death of marriage, only the most flagrant scoundrel would refuse to acknowledge and provide material support to his children if he was in a publicly recognised relationship with their mother at the time of conception. Now, deadbeat dads are commonplace. In the UK, less than two-thirds of non-resident parents – almost all of them fathers – are paying child support in full.[22] In America, the figure is less than half.[23] Not only are record numbers of children not growing up with a father at home, but many of those children don't even get any money out of these absent men.

Despite the often valiant efforts of single mothers, the data clearly shows that, on average, children without fathers at home do not do as well as other children. As the sociologists Sara McLanahan and Gary D. Sandefur write:

> Children who grow up in a household with only one biological parent are worse off, on average, than children who grow up in a household with both of their biological parents, regardless of the parents' race or educational background, regardless of whether the parents are married when the child is born, and regardless of whether the resident parent remarries.[24]

Fatherlessness is associated with higher incarceration rates for boys,[25] higher rates of teen pregnancy for girls,[26] and a greater likelihood of emotional and behavioural problems for both sexes.[27] This is not only because children are denied the material support their fathers might have given them but also because single mothers are obliged to take on the almost impossible task of doing everything themselves: all of the earning, plus all of the caring, socialising, and disciplining of their children.

Then there's the sometimes malign influence of step-parents – mostly, in practice, stepfathers, since in the vast majority of cases it is mothers who are awarded primary custody, and therefore mothers who are likely to bring a new partner into a young child's home. Evolutionary psychologists refer darkly to a phenomenon known as 'the Cinderella effect': the higher incidences of child abuse by step-parents than by biological parents. The effect is so marked that Steven Pinker has described step-parenthood as 'the strongest risk factor for child abuse ever identified'. A step-parent is forty to one hundred times more likely than a biological parent to kill a child,[28] and stepfathers are also far more likely than genetic fathers to sexually abuse children.

Stepchildren, on average, find home life more stressful than other children do. They leave home younger and are more likely to report that family conflict was their key reason for moving out. They have chronically higher levels of the stress hormone cortisol. They suffer higher mortality in general, not just from step-parent assaults but also due to an increased rate of accidents. Their step-parents devote fewer resources to their care, including nutritional resources, resulting in their having a shorter average height than their peers of the same age. All of this holds true across cultures.[29]

Of course it is sometimes better for children not to live with their genetic fathers, or even have contact with them, particularly if those men are abusive or dangerously unstable. And of course there are plenty of devoted stepfathers and stepmothers who make exceptionally good parents. We are talking about risks here, not absolutes – the presence of a step-parent in a young child's home increases the risk of bad outcomes, but it certainly does not guarantee them. However, the research findings are not promising, and parents are kidding themselves if they think that a divorce or parental separation will have no impact on their children. One particularly egregious case of self-deception was published in the *New York Times* in 2021, in a piece by the legal scholar Lara Bazelon in which she described her own experience of divorce:

> To this day, divorce is portrayed as precarious and grim. Parents whose marriages break apart are made to feel they have failed catastrophically. Divorce is shameful, traumatic and Bad For The Kids.
>
> But I've learned that divorce can also be an act of radical self-love that leaves the whole family better off . . . I divorced my husband not because I didn't love him. I divorced him because I loved myself more.[30]

Whether or not it is an act of 'radical self-love' for one or more of the adults, children do not benefit from the divorce of non-abusive parents. The research is unequivocal on this point.

And while a parent like Bazelon may be able to cushion the blow to her children by paying for therapy, nannies and private schools, most single mothers are not able to do so.

As so often, it is poor women who fare worst in the post-sexual revolution era. For one thing, divorce harms mothers financially. As Lenore Weitzman concludes, from her study of divorce in California: 'For most women and children, divorce means precipitous downward mobility – both economically and socially. The reduction in income brings residential moves and inferior housing, drastically diminished or nonexistent funds for recreation and leisure, and intense pressures due to inadequate time and money.'[31]

And the situation is even worse for mothers who never get married in the first place. A 2019 BBC documentary about homeless single mothers included an interview with the father of one of the toddlers featured in the programme. Both child and mother were living in a hostel run by the local council, heavily in debt, and surviving on welfare benefits. She desperately wanted to get back with her ex, and he would occasionally swing by the hostel to spend time with their son, making vague promises about them one day living together as a family. Addressing the camera, he explained his view of the situation: 'It's always good to spend time with my kid. I wish that I could see him when I want to see him, but I think sometimes you have to prioritise your lifestyle.'[32] Plenty of 'radical self-love' on display from a man who seemed to be fond of his child and ex-girlfriend, but who wasn't willing to make even the most minor sacrifice in order to offer them a stable homelife. And why should he? From his perspective, *she* was the one who had decided not to have an abortion, and so *she* must face the consequences alone.

Which means that she becomes dependent on the state. Here, too, is a social change brought about by a material one. It was the economic boom of the post-war period that made possible the construction of a large welfare state, which then made it feasible – although neither easy nor pleasant – for poor single mothers to survive without support from the fathers of their children.

My friend Mason Hartman compares the modern state to a kind of 'back-up husband'. If called upon, it will feed you, house you, and protect you from violence, but it won't do so especially well. And the state will offer no warmth or companionship alongside these basic necessities. I don't suggest for a moment that this 'back-up husband' ought now to withdraw, because doing so would leave many single mothers and their children destitute. The elaborate system of norms that for centuries held together the taboo on pre-marital sex is now long gone and cannot be readily reconstructed. If the welfare state were to disappear, the result would be misery and mayhem for the most vulnerable members of our society.

But nor do I think that the 'back-up husband' is anything like as good as the real thing. Despite all of our efforts, feminists have not yet found a workable alternative to a system that, as it turned out, did serve a purpose in protecting the interests not only of women but also – crucially – of their children.

A baby and someone

Some people consider the death of marriage to be a good thing, and many of those people are feminists. Opposition to marriage was a common theme in much of the writing of the second wave, with feminists including Andrea Dworkin, Germaine Greer and Kate Millett all arguing for its abolition. 'The institution of marriage is the chief vehicle for the perpetuation of the oppression of women,' insisted the American sociologist Marlene Dixon in 1969, summarising the dominant feminist critique of the time. 'It is through the role of wife that the subjugation of women is maintained.'[33]

But it's no coincidence that most of the feminists who opposed marriage never had children. I've written earlier in this book about the conflict between liberal feminists and radical feminists on issues such as prostitution and porn, issues on which there are clear and important differences between these two feminist traditions. On motherhood, however, the differences have always been paper thin. Both groups have no answer to the question of how women are supposed to reconcile their search for freedom with a condition that necessarily curtails it.

If you value freedom above all else, then you must reject motherhood, since this is a state of being that limits a woman's freedom in almost every possible way – not only during pregnancy but also for the rest of her life, since she will always have obligations to her children, and they will always have obligations to her. It's a connection that is only ever severed in the most dire circumstances.

Feminists have historically succeeded in challenging this restriction on freedom through advocating for greater availability of contraception and abortion, which has been effective up to a point, in that it has allowed women more of a say in when or if they have children. But what about when the children are actually born? Here, we come upon an anti-natalist streak in both liberal and radical feminist traditions that leaves mothers shut out, which means – even with historically low birth rates – that at least three-quarters of women are shut out. Motherhood is discussed in fewer than 3 per cent of papers, journal articles or textbooks on modern gender theory[34] – but then, less than half of tenured female academics have children,[35] which makes the omission somewhat less surprising. The whole topic has slipped out of sight.

And no wonder, since the logic of individualism collapses upon contact with motherhood. The pregnant woman's frame contains two people, neither of them truly autonomous. The unborn baby depends on the mother for survival, and the mother cannot break this physical bond except through medical intervention that will result in the baby's death. Even after birth, the mother–baby dyad remains a unit, tied together both emotionally and physically. And, for many years following birth, the young child cannot be understood as an autonomous individual because, without the devoted care of at least one adult, death is a certainty.

The psychoanalyst and paediatrician Donald Winnicott has written that 'there is no such thing as a baby. There is only a baby and someone.' The writer Leah Libresco Sargeant expands the point:

> The liberal theory of the independent individual as the basic unit of society is full of exceptions . . . It would be fairer to say that dependence is our default state, and self-sufficiency the aberration. Our lives begin and (frequently) end in states of near total dependence, and much of the middle is marked by periods of need.[36]

Some feminists insist that women ought to forego motherhood altogether. Shulamith Firestone, for instance, famously argued in *The Dialectic of Sex*, first published in 1970, that women could never be liberated from patriarchy without liberation from reproduction itself, and thus she suggested that babies ought one day to be gestated outside of the human body. If women cannot participate in reproduction as men do, Firestone argued, then they should not participate at all.

This does work up to a point – for the individual, at least, if not for the species. But it isn't possible to reject dependency altogether because, even if a woman chooses never to have children, she will one day grow old and depend on other people as if she were an infant all over again. Shulamith Firestone herself – having become estranged from her family in later life, and having never married or produced children – spent the final years of her life in a state of profound vulnerability caused by severe mental illness. She was supported for a time by a network of feminist friends and admirers, but eventually the group dissipated, since they were not tied together by blood or marriage, and relationships based on mutual liking or idealism are not as durable as those that entail a lifelong obligation. Firestone was left uncared for, and she died alone in her home aged sixty-seven, with her body left undiscovered for some days. It was assumed by the coroner that she had died of starvation.[37]

A modified version of Winnicott's proclamation could be applied to almost all adults at some stage of their lives: 'there is no such thing as a person. There is only a person and someone.' Acting as that 'someone' means giving away some portion of your freedom, which runs counter to what we're all supposed to want. Many feminists of the second wave described their goal as 'women's liberation' – womankind was in chains, they said, and those chains had to be broken.

And that goal was not without merit, given that women are still too often consigned permanently to the role of 'someone' – always caring, never cared for. But the solution to this problem cannot be individualism, because the whole concept is based on a lie. In a natural human life cycle, we begin as dependent babies, spend a very brief period as relatively independent young adults, before caring for our own dependent children, and then ultimately ending our lives in what Shakespeare called our 'second childishness'.[38] Modern contraception has allowed us to stretch out that young adult stage artificially, giving the illusion that independence is our permanent state. But it isn't – it's nothing more than a blip, which some of us will never experience at all. Either being 'a someone' or needing 'a someone' is our lot as human beings. That means that we have to find a way of being dependent upon one another.

The protection of an ordinary marriage

But dependency continues to present problems for feminism, particularly in relation to motherhood. To the extent that either liberal or radical feminism has offered any hypothetical assistance to mothers, it has been assistance located outside of the family and within the bosom of the fully socialised state. The state as back-up husband is tasked with providing institutional childcare in the form of 24/7 day-care centres, which is an elegantly economical model, since, instead of one mother devoted to one child (wastefully, her own), the back-up husband allocates one worker to many children (efficiently, not her own). Mothers can thus return promptly to the workforce and put their tax revenue towards feeding the day-care engine.

Such a model depends on physically prising apart women from their children, making these two beings as autonomous as possible as quickly as possible. Thus women's freedom is maximised and the mutual dependency of childbearing is resisted, or at least hidden away. What this model doesn't offer women is a way of being physically *with* their children while also being materially and emotionally supported by other adults.

Some feminists have attempted to resolve this problem through the construction of new, family-like structures. In *The Female Eunuch*, for instance, Germaine Greer wrote of 'self-regulating organic families', in which groups of women buy a property together and live communally, with the fathers of their children visiting only occasionally[39] and the role of mother frequently 'deputised' to others. Writing fifty years after Greer, Sophie Lewis advocates in her book *Full Surrogacy Now* for 'gestational communism', in which 'mother–child bonds can more easily be discontinued, handed over, and multiplied.'

The sociologist Nicholas Christakis observes that the idea of collective childrearing was not unique to the radicals of the 1970s:

It has been periodically attempted as a desired social disruption since antiquity. Plato believed that raising children communally would result in children treating all men as their fathers and thus more respectfully. Communist societies have also been associated with collective child-rearing; the family is seen as a threat to state ideology because it fosters a sense of belonging to a family unit, and totalitarian ideology requires that family allegiance be subordinated to allegiance to the party or state.[40]

But, as Christakis writes, 'attempts to fundamentally restructure or minimize the bond between parent and child have very rarely, if ever, endured.' The reasons for this should be obvious: humans are animals, descended from individuals whose offspring survived to adulthood, and natural selection therefore favours attentive mothers.

This means that, when social structures fall away, the result is generally that the person left literally holding the baby is the person whose natural instincts make her most devoted to the child. Shulamith Firestone recognised this truth, writing that: 'Since the relationship "mother/child" remains intact, it is no wonder that when the commune breaks up, all the "godparents" disappear, as well as the genetic father himself, leaving the mother stuck – without even the protection of an ordinary marriage.' Firestone's argument, of course, is that even communal childrearing does not free women from the oppression of motherhood, and that the whole thing should therefore be rejected. But the phrase 'without even the protection of an ordinary marriage' is well put. The reductive feminist analysis of marriage sees it as a method used by men to control female sexuality. And it does do that, of course, but that was never its sole function. There is also a protective function to marriage, but it's one that makes sense only when understood in relation to children.

The faithless soldier

Marriage used to be defined as a conjugal union, 'a holy mystery in which man and woman become one flesh', in the words of the marriage service of the Church of England. While of course there were always exceptions to this infertile people were permitted to marry, as were people beyond reproductive age – marriage was nevertheless understood to be based, as Robert P. George, professor of jurisprudence at Princeton, puts it, around a couple's 'sexual-reproductive complementarity . . . [which was] specially apt for, and would naturally be fulfilled by, their having and rearing children together.'[41]

For most Westerners, this is no longer what marriage means. The psychologist Eli Finkel has charted the historical development of marriage in the Western world and attributes its changes to changing economic conditions.[42] Before the mid-nineteenth century, the challenge of day-to-day survival, particularly for rural people, meant that assistance with food production, shelter, and protection from violence were what most people prioritised in a spouse. Later, urbanisation and industrialisation led to greater prosperity, and couples had the luxury in their marriages of placing more emphasis on love and companionship. Then, in the affluent 1960s, we entered the era of what Finkel refers to as the 'self-expressive marriage', in which self-discovery, self-esteem and personal growth became the key markers of a marriage's success.

Where once marriage was all about reproduction and the pooling of resources, it is now more often understood as a means of sexual and emotional fulfilment – 'your relationship with your Number One person',[43] as the philosopher John Corvino has put it. Thus it is now perfectly intelligible – and, in my opinion, good and proper – to extend marriage rights to same-sex couples, who necessarily lack 'sexual-reproductive complementarity'. Since the old meaning of marriage is now forgotten, denying same-sex couples the right to marry in the present day is both cruel and nonsensical.

But we should not make the mistake of misrepresenting the historical function of marriage, and indeed the historical function of the prohibition on pre-marital sex. Modern feminists who have only ever known a world with the Pill can easily forget that, in an era without contraception, a prohibition on sex before marriage served *female*, not male interests, because it protected the group of people who bear (literally) the consequences of an extramarital pregnancy.

This point was well understood by feminists who were born long before the Pill's invention and who knew what an extramarital pregnancy meant for a woman in a society without a welfare state. Yes, it's true that part of the harm was done through reputational damage, with single mothers and their children stigmatised by their families and communities. But this social catastrophe was second order to the practical catastrophe of *single motherhood itself*, which was disastrous enough to result, for some poor women, in a choice between prostitution and starvation, or else other alternatives that were just as terrible: a dangerous attempt at abortion, abandonment of a child to an orphanage or infanticide. The stigma around single motherhood caused a great deal of misery for its many victims. It also existed for a reason: to deter women from making an irreparable mistake for the sake of a worthless man.

The feminist theorist Mary Harrington uncovers the logic of the old prohibition on extramarital sex within English folksongs about the 'faithless soldier' and the young woman he seduces:

> Cold Blow and the Rainy Night tells of a soldier who arrives, hat frozen to his head, pleading with a young woman to let him in. She's eventually persuaded, whereupon one thing leads to another. Presumably in the afterglow, she asks him: 'Now since

you had your will of me / Soldier will you marry me?'. Nope,
he replies:

> O then she cursed the rainy night
> That ever she let him in – O
> Then he jumped out of the bed
> He put his cap upon his head
> And she had lost her maidenhead
> And her mother heard the din – O
>
> . . .

Another song, The Greenwood Side, recounts the story of a
young woman who falls pregnant in an illicit affair, is abandoned by her lover, gives birth alone in a wood and conceals the
truth by murdering her twin babies. The affair, abandonment,
birth and infanticide are briskly narrated, and the body of the
song is a hallucinated dialogue with her murdered babies. The
deeply unsettling lyrics blend horror at her deed with profound
pity for the woman:

> Now, bonny boys, come tell to me
> Oh, the rose and the linsey, oh
> What sort of life I'll have after dying?
> Down by the Greenwood side, oh[44]

Such songs existed to warn young women about the dangers
posed by the faithless soldier and his kind. What might nowadays be interpreted as 'slut shaming', or a fear of female sexual
agency, in fact had a very urgent purpose. That purpose is
now somewhat anachronistic in an age of contraception, but
only somewhat. Illicit affairs *do still* end in trauma and tragedy
because sex *is still* just as consequential as it ever was.

Many feminists who lived before the 1960s knew this better
than we do now. They looked at the asymmetries inherent
in heterosexuality and the grim consequences for women of
'sexual liberation', and they concluded that the male libido
needed containment. Which was why two of the thirteen

chapters in Mary Wollstonecraft's *A Vindication of the Rights of Woman* were devoted to bemoaning the lack of chastity in men – the sex with the higher sex drive – and thus – to Wollstonecraft's mind – the greater responsibility for containing their passions. 'Votes for women, chastity for men' was a real suffragist slogan, now forgotten.[45]

The reinvention of marriage

But how to persuade men into – if not chastity – sexual continence? I've written earlier in this book about what I've called the 'cad' and 'dad' modes of male sexuality, with the former orientated towards casual sex and the latter towards commitment. Although there are some men who are innately and resolutely focused on one or other of these modes, it's far more common for men to sit somewhere in the middle, moving between the two depending on their age and social context.

Having almost reached the end of this book, I hope I've managed to persuade you that the cad mode of male sexuality is bad for women en masse. The vast majority of women find it difficult to detach emotion from sex, meaning that an encounter with a cad who doesn't call is likely to leave a woman feeling distressed, even if she attempts to repress those feelings. Women did not evolve to treat sex as meaningless, and trying to pretend otherwise does not end well.

Then there are the physical consequences of sex, which are inherently asymmetrical, with the danger and pain of an unwanted pregnancy borne entirely by the woman. Modern forms of contraception are mostly effective – enough, at least, to have transformed sexual relations in the post-1960s era – but they still regularly fail. And whatever you think about the ethical status of the foetus, we should all be able to agree that an abortion is not a good thing for a woman to go through, given such medical risks as uterine damage or sepsis, not to mention the emotional consequences, which are not trivial.

All in all, attempting to mimic the cad mode of male sexuality, as liberal feminism encourages, does not constitute liberation for women. The Hugh Hefners of the world do not quail at the thought of a 'sexually liberated' woman kind. Quite the opposite, in fact. They are delighted to find themselves with a buffet of young women to feast on, all of them apparently willing to suffer their mistreatment without complaint. Looked at in the starkest terms, I can't help but agree with the dark pronouncement my grandmother made when I told her about the thesis of this book: 'women have been conned.'

The task for practically minded feminists, then, is to deter men from cad mode. Our current sexual culture does not do that, but it could. In order to change the incentive structure, we would need a technology that discourages short-termism in male sexual behaviour, protects the economic interests of mothers, and creates a stable environment for the raising of children. And we do already have such a technology, even if it is old, clunky and prone to periodic failure. It's called monogamous marriage.

Before I start sounding too quixotic, I should make one thing clear: lifelong monogamy is not our natural state. Only about 15 per cent of societies in the anthropological record have been monogamous.[46] Monogamy has to be enforced through laws and customs, and, even within societies in which it is deeply embedded, plenty of people are defiant. To date, monogamy has been dominant in only two types of society: small-scale groups beset by serious environmental privation and some of the most complex civilisations to have ever existed, including our own.[47] Almost all others have been polygynous, permitting high-status men to take multiple wives.

But while the monogamous marriage model may be relatively unusual, it is also spectacularly successful. When monogamy is imposed on a society, it tends to become richer. It has lower rates of both child abuse and domestic violence, since conflict between co-wives tends to generate both. Birth rates and crime rates both fall, which encourages economic development, and wealthy men, denied the opportunity to devote their resources to acquiring more wives, instead invest elsewhere: in property, businesses, employees, and other productive endeavours.

This is, it seems, the solution to what anthropologists have called 'the puzzle of monogamous marriage'. How is it that a marriage system that does not suit the interests of the most powerful members of society – high-status men – has nevertheless come to be institutionalised across so much of the world? The answer is that, although monogamy is less satisfactory for these men, it produces wealthy, stable societies that survive.

A monogamous marriage system is successful in part because it pushes men away from cad mode, particularly when pre-marital sex is also prohibited. Under these circumstances, if a man wants to have sex in a way that's socially acceptable, he has to make himself marriageable, which means holding down a good job and setting up a household suitable for the raising of children. He has to tame himself, in other words. Fatherhood then has a further taming effect, even at the biochemical level: when men are involved in the care of their young children, their testosterone levels drop, alongside their aggression and sex drive.[48] A society composed of tamed men is a better society to live in, for men, for women and for children.

The monogamous marriage model is also the best solution yet discovered to the problems presented by childrearing. There was a wisdom to the traditional model in which the father was primarily responsible for earning money while the mother was primarily responsible for caring for children at home. Such a model allows mothers and children to be physically together and at the same time financially supported. In an age of labour-saving devices such as washing machines and gas boilers, it has become less time-consuming to run a household and thus more feasible for mothers of young children to do paid work outside of the home, as most of us do. But attempting to play the traditional roles of mother and father simultaneously – as single mothers are forced to do – is close to impossible.

For some women, paid work outside of the home is a joy and a privilege. For many more, it is a responsibility, and often an onerous one. Even those women who enjoy their work are physically incapable of performing it during the early months of a baby's life. I should know: I began this book at the beginning of my pregnancy and completed it when my son was six months old. Writing is probably one of the easiest jobs to combine with motherhood, but even so there were weeks on end during which I didn't write a word because I was too busy caring for my baby. And while I could be practically supported by other people, including my husband, I was irreplaceable as mother – not only because I was the only person who could breastfeed, but also because children have a relationship with their mothers that starts from conception, and that relationship cannot be handed over without distress to both mother and baby.

If we want to keep that maternal bond intact, then the only solution is for another person to step in during these times of vulnerability and do the tasks needed to keep a household warm and fed. Perhaps we could call that person a spouse. Perhaps we could call their legal and emotional bond a marriage.

Marriage is an institution that has a way of reinventing itself. In 2020, an initiative set up by a group of American students called the Affirmative Consent Project began marketing a 'consent kit', available online for $2.99. This pocket-sized kit contained a condom, two breath mints, and a contract stating that the undersigned had agreed to have sex. Couples were encouraged to take a photo of themselves holding the signed piece of paper. ('Why not invite family and friends to witness the signing?' some wags asked. 'Why not hire a professional photographer? Dress up? Make an event of it?')[49]

Similarly, in 2021, the journalist Julia Ioffe was among the many feminists who responded to the introduction of new restrictions on abortion rights in Texas by suggesting that men ought to be compelled to provide financial support to their sexual partners if they became pregnant. Ioffe tweeted, apparently expecting conservatives to be outraged by this extremely conservative proposal: 'If you are anti-choice and you want to make sure women carry every pregnancy to term, why not make the person who created the pregnancy contribute? Why not have men pay child support to the women they impregnate?'[50] Why not indeed? In fact I'd say that it's quite possible to be pro-choice *and* to insist that men ought to take responsibility for the children they help to create. We used to have a social institution established for exactly that purpose. We still could.

I have just one piece of advice to offer in this chapter, and you've probably already guessed what it will be. So, here it is: get married. And do your best to stay married. Particularly if you have children, and particularly if those children are still young. And if you do find yourself in the position of being a single mother, wait until your children are older before you bring a stepfather into their home. These directives are harder to follow now than they used to be, because we no longer live in a culture that incentivises perseverance in marriage. But it is still possible for individuals to go against the grain and insist on doing the harder, less fashionable thing.

The critics of marriage are right to say that it has historically been used as a vehicle for the control of women by men, and they're right to point out that most marriages do not live up to a romantic ideal. They're right, too, that monogamous, lifelong marriage is in a sense 'unnatural' in that it is not the human norm. The marriage system that prevailed in the West up until recently was not perfect, nor was it easy for most people to conform to, since it demanded high levels of tolerance and self-control. Where the critics go wrong is in arguing that there is any better system. There isn't.

Conclusion:
Listen to Your Mother

I'm treading a fine line in this book. On the one hand, I'm arguing against a naive kind of 'choice feminism' that fails to acknowledge the subtle and not so subtle incentive structures that influence individual decision making. On the other hand, I'm trying to encourage readers to make particular choices, fully in the knowledge that your agency is heavily constrained. In other words, I'm telling you that your options are limited but that you do still have them. 'There are ways out,' as the poet Charles Bukowski puts it, 'there is light somewhere, it may not be much light, but it beats the darkness.'

So I've tried to offer chinks of light. Because I truly believe not only that there is scope for individuals to behave differently, but also that these individual actions can scale to something more significant. Things can change very quickly when people realise that there are others who secretly feel the same way as they do.

My friend the writer Katherine Dee has been predicting a change for some time. 'I believe the pendulum with sexuality is going to swing, big time,' she wrote last year. 'We're diving headlong into something that's been simmering in the background since 2013–2014 . . . The pot is about to boil over.'

Katherine is one of those people who has a talent for noticing changes in the cultural winds, and she observes more and more signs of a coming reaction against the excesses of the sexual liberation narrative, particularly from Gen Z women who have experienced the worst of it.[1]

I think Katherine is right on this. And while I wrote this book in the hope that it would be read by men and women of all ages, my dearest wish is that it will be read by young women in particular – the group who have been utterly failed by liberal feminism and who have the most to gain from a swing back against its excesses.

So while there is advice within these pages that could be helpful to any reader, it is worth repeating here the points that are most relevant to these particular young women. This is the same advice I would offer my own daughter:

• Distrust any person or ideology that puts pressure on you to ignore your moral intuition.
• Chivalry is actually a good thing. We all have to control our sexual desires, and men particularly so, given their greater physical strength and average higher sex drives.
• Sometimes (though not always) you can readily spot sexually aggressive men. There are a handful of personality traits that are common to them: impulsivity, promiscuity, hyper-masculinity and disagreeableness. These traits in combination should put you on your guard.
• A man who is aroused by violence is a man to steer well clear of, whether or not he uses the vocabulary of BDSM to excuse his behaviour. If he can maintain an erection while beating a woman, he isn't safe to be alone with.
• Consent workshops are mostly useless. The best way of reducing the incidence of rape is by reducing the opportunities for would-be rapists to offend. This can be done either by keeping convicted rapists in prison or by limiting their access to potential victims.

- The category of people most likely to become victims of these men are young women aged about thirteen to twenty-five. All girls and women, but particularly those in this age category, should avoid being alone with men they don't know or men who give them the creeps. Gut instinct is not to be ignored: it's usually triggered by a red flag that's well worth noticing.
- Get drunk or high in private and with female friends rather than in public or in mixed company.
- Don't use dating apps. Mutual friends can vet histories and punish bad behaviour. Dating apps can't.
- Holding off on having sex with a new boyfriend for at least a few months is a good way of discovering whether or not he's serious about you or just looking for a hook-up.
- Only have sex with a man if you think he would make a good father to your children – not because you necessarily intend to have children with him, but because this is a good rule of thumb in deciding whether or not he's worthy of your trust.
- Monogamous marriage is by far the most stable and reliable foundation on which to build a family.

I wrote in the first chapter that none of my advice would be ground-breaking, and I stand by that. This is all informed by peer-reviewed research, but it shouldn't have to be, since this is pretty much what most mothers would tell their daughters, if only they were willing to listen.

If we are to challenge the social costs of the sexual revolution effectively, then we can't redesign society on the back of an envelope. We have to look at social structures that have already proven to be successful in the past and compare them against one another, rather than against some imagined alternative that has never existed and is never likely to exist. The technology shock of the Pill led sexual liberals to the hubristic assumption that our society could be uniquely free from the oppression of sexual norms and could function just fine.

The last sixty years have proved that assumption to be wrong. We need to re-erect the social guard rails that have been torn down. And, in order to do that, we have to start by stating the obvious. Sex must be taken seriously. Men and women are different. Some desires are bad. Consent is not enough. Violence is not love. Loveless sex is not empowering. People are not products. Marriage is good.

And, above all, listen to your mother. In 2021, a TikTok video by a young American woman called Abby went viral online. In the video, Abby tells the camera:

> I, like many other college students, am someone who is entangled in hook-up culture, and often hook-up culture makes it difficult for me to determine whether or not what I'm doing is good for me and kind to myself. Very often as women we are led astray from what we actually deserve. So here's what I've been doing lately . . .

She pulls up on screen a series of childhood photos of herself and explains that the men she's hooked up with in the past have often made her feel as though she's undeserving, not only of love but also of basic respect. So she's trying to remind herself of her worth as a person by playing the role of mother to her inner child. 'Am I OK with that for her?', she asks tearfully, gesturing at her younger self in the photo. 'Would I let her be a late-night, drunk second option? Would I let this happen to her?' She shakes her head, weeping: 'From a third person, caretaker point of view, I would never let any of this stuff happen to her.'[2]

Abby is trying to mother herself, though she isn't quite sure how to do it. And the thousands of young women in her replies are trying to do the same ('I'm sobbing'; 'i rlly needed this, thank you'; 'this just changed my life'). They've been denied the guidance of mothers, not because their actual mothers are unwilling to offer it but because of a matricidal impulse in

liberal feminism that cuts young women off from the 'problematic' older generation. This means not only that they are
cut off from the voices of experience, but – more importantly
– they are also cut off from the person who loves them most in
the world. Feminism needs to rediscover the mother, in every
sense.

Until we do, each individual woman will have to learn on
her own the lie of the promise of sexual liberation – the lie that
tells us, as Andrea Dworkin phrased it, that 'fucking per se is
freedom per se.' It was a lie all along. It's time, at last, to say so.

Notes

Chapter 1 Sex Must Be Taken Seriously

1 Gianluca Mezzofiore, 'No, that viral picture doesn't show Hugh Hefner lighting a cigarette for Marilyn Monroe', 28 September 2017, https://mashable.com/2017/09/28/marilyn-monroe-hugh-hefner-fake-picture-playboy/?europe=true.

2 Jack Shepherd, 'Hugh Hefner dead: Playboy founder is being buried next to Marilyn Monroe', 28 September 2017, www.independent.co.uk/arts-entertainment/films/news.

3 Jeff Gottlieb, 'For sale: eternity with Marilyn Monroe', 14 August 2009, www.latimes.com/archives/la-xpm-2009-aug-14-me-marilyn14-story.html.

4 Brad Witter, 'Marilyn Monroe didn't actually pose for the first issue of Playboy', 8 September 2020, www.biography.com/news/marilyn-monroe-playboy-first-issue-didnt-pose.

5 Scott Johnson, 4 October 2017, www.hollywoodreporter.com/news/playboys-first-black-playmate-reflects-hugh-hefners-legacy-1045838.

6 Witter, 'Marilyn Monroe didn't actually pose'.

7 'Hugh Hefner will be buried next to Marilyn Monroe', 29 September 2017, www.telegraph.co.uk/films/2017/09/29/hugh-hefner-buried-next-marilyn-monroe-fans-not-happy/.

8　Megan C. Hills, 'How Hugh Hefner built an entire empire without Marilyn Monroe's consent', 29 September 2017, www.marieclaire.co.uk/news/celebrity-news/hugh-hefner-marilyn-monroe-541688.

9　Andrea Dworkin, *Right-Wing Women*. New York: Perigee Books, [1978] 1983, p. 18.

10　Corita Grudzen, Daniella Meeker, Jacqueline Torres et al., 'Comparison of the mental health of female adult film performers and other young women in California', *Psychiatric Services* 62 (2011): 639–45.

11　Sam Kashner, 'Marilyn and her monsters', 5 October 2010, www.vanityfair.com/culture/2010/11/marilyn-monroe-201011.

12　'Hugh Hefner quotes', 28 September 2017, https://heavy.com/entertainment/2017/09/hugh-hefner-quotes-on-life-death-playboy-is-alive-dead/.

13　Olivia Bahou, 11 June 2015, www.cosmopolitan.com/sex-love/news/a41845/worst-things-playmates-said-about-playboy-mansion/.

14　Ibid.

15　Sharon Waxman, 28 September 2017, www.thewrap.com/hugh-hefner-legacy-no-feminist-hero/.

16　Graeme Culliford, 'Sickening pimp secret', 2 October 2017, www.thesun.co.uk/news/4585472/brit-model-lured-girls-to-the-playboy-mansion-to-have-orgies-with-hugh-hefner/.

17　Brooks Barnes, 'The loin in winter', 23 October 2009, www.nytimes.com/2009/10/24/business/media/24hefner.html?pagewanted=2&sq=hefner&st=cse&scp=1.

18　Emma Gray, 'The contradictory feminist legacy of Playboy's Hugh Hefner', 29 September 2017, www.huffingtonpost.co.uk/entry/playboy-hugh-hefner-feminist-contradiction_n_59cd07c4e4b0210dfdfc822d?ri18n=true.

19　Nalina Eggert, 'Hugh Hefner death: was the Playboy revolution good for women?', 28 September 2017, www.bbc.co.uk/news/world-us-canada-41426299.

20　Pascale Day, 'Opinion', 28 September 2017, https://metro.co.uk

/2017/09/28/hugh-hefner-might-have-been-a-sleaze-but-play
boy-helped-push-feminism-forwards-6963213/?ito=cbshare.

21 Patrick J. Deneen, June 2015, www.firstthings.com/article/2015
/06/the-power-elite.

22 See www.theguardian.com/film/2017/mar/05/emma-watson-va
nity-fair-cover-feminism.

23 Thanks to the American writer Aaron Sibarium for coining the
term 'sexual disenchantment' here: see https://americancompass
.org/the-commons/three-theses-about-cuties/.

24 https://medium.com/@totalsratmove?p=2194a96bdbb6.

25 Jessica Valenti, '#MeToo is about more than stopping rape', 31
January 2018, www.theguardian.com/commentisfree/2018/jan
/31/me-too-we-demand-more-jessica-valenti.

26 Jessica Valenti and Jaclyn Friedman, *Believe Me: How Trusting
Women Can Change the World*. New York: Basic Books.

27 https://en.wikipedia.org/wiki/List_of_universities_with_BDSM
_clubs.

28 https://en.wikipedia.org/wiki/Sex_Week_at_Yale.

29 Allie Grasgreen, 'Fifty shades of crimson', 5 December 2012,
www.insidehighered.com/news/2012/12/05/kink-clubs-harvar
ds-well-established-healthy-students.

30 C. S. Lewis, *Surprised by Joy*. London: HarperCollins, 2012.

31 See www.glamour.com/story/12-friends-moments-that-will-to
tally-make-you-cringe-now.

32 Laura House, 'Plan dinner the night before, NEVER complain
and speak in a soft voice', 7 December 2016, www.dailymail.co
.uk/femail/article-4011366/Cringeworthy-1950s-marriage-advi
ce-teaching-housewives-look-husbands.html.

33 www.cosmopolitan.com/sex-love/advice/g3765/ways-to-please
-a-man/.

34 www.cosmopolitan.com/uk/love-sex/sex/tips/g1508/turn-him
-on-sex-tips/.

35 www.cosmopolitan.com/sex-love/confessions/advice/g1788
/how-to-turn-him-on/.

Chapter 2 Men and Women Are Different

1 Randy Thornhill and Craig T. Palmer, *A Natural History of Rape: Biological Bases of Sexual Coercion*. Chicago: MIT Press, 2000.

2 Alice Dreger, *Galileo's Middle Finger: Heretics, Activists, and One Scholar's Search for Justice*. New York: Penguin, p. 124.

3 See www.nypl.org/voices/print-publications/books-of-the-century.

4 Susan Brownmiller, *Against Our Will: Men, Women and Rape*. New York: Simon & Schuster, 1975, p. 6 [Kindle locations 238–9].

5 Jill Filipovic, 29 August 2013, www.theguardian.com/commentisfree/2013/aug/29/rape-about-power-not-sex.

6 Brownmiller, *Against Our Will* [Kindle locations 92–3].

7 Cordelia Fine, *Delusions of Gender*. Cambridge: Icon, 2013, p. 198.

8 Brownmiller, *Against Our Will* [Kindle location 199].

9 John MacKinnon, 'The orang-utan in Sabah today', *Oryx* 11 (1971): 141–91, at p. 175.

10 B. M. F. Galdikas, *Reflections of Eden: My Life with the Orangutans of Borneo*. London: Indigo, 1996; John C. Mitani, 'Mating behaviour of male orangutans in the Kutai Game Reserve, Indonesia', *Animal Behaviour* 33 (1985): 392–402.

11 Thornhill and Palmer, *A Natural History of Rape*, pp. 82–3.

12 Sarah Blaffer Hrdy, *Mother Nature: A History of Mothers, Infants, and Natural Selection*. New York: Pantheon, 1999.

13 A. E. Miller, J. D. MacDougall, M. A. Tarnopolsky and D. G. Sale, 'Gender differences in strength and muscle fiber characteristics', *European Journal of Applied Physiology and Occupational Physiology* 66 (1993): 254–62.

14 Tal Amasay, Constance M. Mier, Katelyn K. Foley and Tonya L. Carswell, 'Gender differences in performance of equivalently loaded push-up and bench-press exercises', *Journal of Sport* 5 (2016): 46–63.

15 Paul Gabrielsen, 'Why males pack a powerful punch', 5 February 2020, https://phys.org/news/2020-02-males-powerful.html.

16 D. Leyk, W. Gorges, D. Ridder et al., 'Hand-grip strength of

young men, women and highly trained female athletes', *European Journal of Applied Physiology* 99 (2007): 415–21.

17 Robinson Meyer, 7 August 2012, www.theatlantic.com/technolo gy/archive/2012/08/the-golden-ratio-the-one-number-that-des cribes-how-mens-world-records-compare-with-womens/260 758/.

18 See https://en.wikipedia.org/wiki/CARIFTA_Games#Boys_Un der_17.

19 See www.truthorfiction.com/was-the-u-s-womens-national-te am-defeated-by-teenaged-boys-in-a-2017-soccer-match/.

20 See www.newstatesman.com/politics/sport/2016/07/olympics -one-question-will-hang-over-female-athletes-are-you-real-wo man.

21 'Dame Kelly Holmes, Paula Radcliffe and Sharron Davies to write to IOC over transgender athletes', 18 March 2019, www.bbc.co .uk/sport/47608623.

22 Sean Ingle, 3 March 2019, https://www.theguardian.com/society /2019/mar/03/sports-stars-weigh-in-on-row-over-transgender -athletes.

23 Aaron Sell, Aaron W. Lukazsweski and Michael Townsley, 'Cues of upper body strength account for most of the variance in men's bodily attractiveness', *Proceedings of the Royal Society B: Biological Sciences* 284 (2017), https://royalsocietypublishing.org /doi/10.1098/rspb.2017.1819.

24 'Google's ideological echo chamber', July 2017, https://web.arch ive.org/web/20170809021151/https://diversitymemo.com/.

25 Paul Lewis, 'I see things differently', 17 November 2017, www.th eguardian.com/technology/2017/nov/16/james-damore-google -memo-interview-autism-regrets.

26 'Google's ideological echo chamber'.

27 See www.youtube.com/watch?v=wTHgMxQEoPI.

28 Camilla Turner, 26 November 2020, www.telegraph.co.uk/ne ws/2020/11/26/exclusive-eton-college-dismisses-teacher-amid -free-speech-row/.

29 Richard B. Felson and Patrick R. Cundiff, 'Sexual assault as a

crime against young people', *Archives of Sexual Behavior* 43 (2014): 273–84.

30 Thornhill and Palmer, *A Natural History of Rape*, p. 72.

31 Richard Felson and Richard Moran, 2 January 2016, https://quil lette.com/2016/01/02/to-rape-is-to-want-sex-not-power/.

32 T. A. Gannon, R. M. Collie, T. Ward and J. Thakker, 'Rape: psychopathology, theory and treatment', *Clinical Psychology Review* 28 (2008): 982–1008.

33 Thornhill and Palmer, *A Natural History of Rape*, p. 134.

34 Richard Wrangham and Dale Peterson, *Demonic Males: Apes and the Origins of Human Violence*. London: Bloomsbury, 1997, p. 140.

35 Dreger, *Galileo's Middle Finger*, pp. 118–20.

36 David Buss, *The Evolution of Desire: Strategies of Human Mating*. New York: Basic Books, [1994] 2016, p. 256.

37 Dina McMillan, 13 April 2018, https://singjupost.com/unmaski ng-the-abuser-dina-mcmillan-at-tedxcanberra-full-transcript/.

38 Thornhill and Palmer, *A Natural History of Rape*, p. 76.

39 Buss, *The Evolution of Desire*, p. 256.

40 'Sussex Police defends "victim blaming" campaign poster', 8 April 2015, www.bbc.co.uk/news/uk-england-sussex-32216176.

41 See www.change.org/p/sussex-police-withdraw-your-rape-pre vention-posters-which-blames-victims-of-sexual-assault.

42 'Sex offender treatment scheme led to increase in reoffending', 30 June 2017, www.theguardian.com/ uk-news/2017/jun/30/ sex-offenders-on-group-treatment-programme-more-likely-to-reoffend.

Chapter 3 Not All Desires Are Good

1 Jonathan Haidt, *The Righteous Mind: Why Good People Are Divided by Politics and Religion*. London: Allen Lane, 2012, pp. 170–6.

2 Richard Guy Parker and Peter Aggleton, eds, *Culture, Society and Sexuality: A Reader*. London: Psychology Press, 1999, p. 171.

3 R. H. Tawney, *Equality*. 4th edn, London: Allen & Unwin, [1931] 1952, pp. 181–2.

4 David P. Schmitt, 'Sociosexuality from Argentina to Zimbabwe: a 48-nation study of sex, culture, and strategies of human mating', *Behavioral and Brain Sciences* 28 (2005): 247–75; discussion, 275–311.

5 S. J. Dawson, B. A. Bannerman and M. L. Lalumière, 'Paraphilic interests: an examination of sex differences in a nonclinical sample', *Sexual Abuse* 28 (2016): 20–45.

6 See www.bsa.natcen.ac.uk/latest-report/british-social-attitudes -30/personal-relationships/homosexuality.aspx.

7 https://en.wikipedia.org/wiki/Legal_status_of_same-sex_marria ge.

8 Andrew Sullivan, 28 August 1989, https://newrepublic.com/arti cle/79054/here-comes-the-groom.

9 G. K. Chesterton, *The Thing: Why I Am a Catholic*. London: Sheed & Ward, 1929, ch. 4.

10 Raymond Williams, *Marxism and Literature*. Oxford: Oxford University Press, 1977.

11 Ben Thompson, 'Ban this filth!', 9 November 2012, https://web.ar chive.org/web/20121112141447/http://www.ft.com/cms/s/2/09 3c3726-24e1-11e2-86fb-00144feabdc0.html#axzz2Bv5X322utv %23axzz2Bv5X3utv.

12 Geoffrey Robertson, 24 May 2008, www.thetimes.co.uk/article /the-mary-whitehouse-story-mary-quite-contrary-dgqdtrf2q xq.

13 Mary Kenny, 'In defence of Mary Whitehouse', 7 June 2010, www.spectator.co.uk/article/in-defence-of-mary-whitehouse.

14 See www.theguardian.com/commentisfree/video/2020/sep/22 /from-mary-whitehouse-to-the-proms-owen-jones-on-how-wo ke-became-a-dirty-word-video.

15 Daniel Boffey, 'Revealed: how Jimmy Savile abused up to 1,000 victims on BBC premises', 18 January 2014, www.theguardian .com/media/2014/jan/18/jimmy-savile-abused-1000-victims -bbc.

16 See https://order-order.com/2012/10/02/piers-morgan-laughed-off-saviles-underage-sex-joke/.

17 John F. Burns and Ravi Somaiya, 2 November 2012, www.nytimes.com/2012/11/02/world/europe/shield-of-celebrity-protected-savile-for-decades.html?auth=login-smartlock.

18 Louis Theroux, 'Looking back on Jimmy Savile', 1 October 2016, www.bbc.co.uk/news/magazine-37517619.

19 Scott D'Arcy and Dan Bloom, 'Paedophile Information Exchange: Leon Brittan "opposed banning pro-child sex campaign group"', 4 June 2015, www.mirror.co.uk/news/uk-news/paedophile-information-exchange-leon-brittan-5825108.

20 Tim Stanley, 1 March 2014, https://web.archive.org/web/20140306014809/http://blogs.telegraph.co.uk/news/timstanley/100261734/allen-ginsberg-camille-paglia-and-the-literary-champions-of-paedophilia/.

21 See https://en.wikipedia.org/wiki/Color_Climax_Corporation.

22 See www.rt.com/news/child-porn-in-open-access-at-swedish-national-library/.

23 See https://en.wikipedia.org/wiki/French_petition_against_age_of_consent_laws.

24 Matthew Campbell, 28 March 2021, www.thetimes.co.uk/article/french-philosopher-michel-foucault-abused-boys-in-tunisia-6t5sj7jvw.

25 Louise Griffin, 13 January 2021, https://metro.co.uk/2021/01/13/belle-delphine-responds-as-shes-accused-of-fetishising-rape-13894142/?ito=cbshare.

26 See https://twitter.com/RepJimBanks/status/1304556525789351937.

27 For reviews, see www.washingtonpost.com/opinions/2020/09/11/people-freaking-out-about-cuties-should-try-it-they-might-find-lot-like/; www.rollingstone.com/movies/movie-reviews/cuties-movie-review-1056197/; www.newyorker.com/culture/the-front-row/cuties-mignonnes-the-extraordinary-netflix-debut-that-became-the-target-of-a-right-wing-campaign; www.telegraph.co.uk/films/0/cuties-netflix-reviewa-provocative-powder-keg-age-terrified/.

28 See www.pressgazette.co.uk/a-tale-told-too-much-the-paediat rician-vigilantes/.

29 Patrick Califia, *Public Sex: The Culture of Radical Sex*. San Francisco: Cleis Press, 2000, p. 26.

30 Matthew Sweet, *Inventing the Victorians*. London: Faber & Faber, 2002.

31 Francesca Bacardi, 14 January 2021, https://pagesix.com/2021 /01/14/armie-hammers-ex-courtney-vucekovich-he-wanted-to -barbecue-and-eat-me/.

32 Mike Vulpo, 26 January 2021, www.eonline.com/news/1231009 /armie-hammers-ex-paige-lorenze-details-their-polyamorous -bdsm-relationship.

33 Natasha Preskey, 20 March 2021, www.independent.co.uk/life -style/armie-hammer-dms-sex-interviews-b1787196.html.

34 Katie Way, 'I went on a date with Aziz Ansari', https://babe.net /2018/01/13/aziz-ansari-28355.

35 Mary Harrington, 'Feminism against progress' (2021), unpublished manuscript.

Chapter 4 Loveless Sex Is Not Empowering

1 Elaine McCahill, 'There's a tension', 29 September 2016, www .thesun.co.uk/tvandshowbiz/1880453/the-falls-gillian-anderson discusses sexual chemistry between her character and jamie -dornans-serial-killer/.

2 Karley Sciortino, *Slutever: Dispatches from a Sexually Autonomous Woman in a Post-Shame World*. New York: Grand Central, 2018, pp. 10–11.

3 'The revised sociosexual orientation inventory (SOI-R) short manual', www.larspenke.eu/pdfs/SOI-R%20Manual.pdf.

4 David P. Schmitt, 'Sociosexuality from Argentina to Zimbabwe: a 48-nation study of sex, culture, and strategies of human mating', *Behavioral and Brain Sciences* 28 (2005): 247–75; discussion, 275–311.

5 Anne Campbell, *A Mind of Her Own: The Evolutionary Psychology of Women*. 2nd edn, Oxford: Oxford University Press, [2002] 2013, p. 51.

6 J. V. Bailey, C. Farquhar, C. Owen et al., 'Sexual behaviour of lesbians and bisexual women', *Sexually Transmitted Infections* 79 (2003): 147–50.

7 L. Henderson, D. Reid, F. Hickson et al., *First, Service Relationships, Sex and Health amongst Lesbian and Bisexual Women*. London: Sigma Research, 2001; https://researchonline.lshtm.ac.uk/id/ep rint/1402.

8 See www.economist.com/britain/2020/01/09/why-lesbian-coup les-are-more-likely-to-divorce-than-gay-ones.

9 Andrew Sullivan, *Love Undetectable: Notes on Friendship, Sex, and Survival*. New York: Alfred A. Knopf, 1998, pp. 162–3.

10 Ibid., p. 160.

11 *Partnership Patterns and HIV Prevention amongst Men who have Sex with Men (MSM)*, www.nat.org.uk/sites/default/files/pub lications/July-2010-Partnership-Patterns-and-HIV-Prevention .pdf.

12 Ford Hickson et al., *Testing Targets: Findings from the United Kingdom Gay Men's Sex Survey 2007*, https://researchonline.lsh tm.ac.uk/id/eprint/1386840/1/report2009f.pdf.

13 Catherine H. Mercer et al., 'The health and well-being of men who have sex with men (MSM) in Britain: evidence from the third National Survey of Sexual Attitudes and Lifestyles (Natsal-3)', *BMC Public Health* 16 (2016), article 525; doi:10.1186/s128 89-016-3149-z.

14 R. D. Clark and E. Hatfield, 'Gender differences in receptivity to sexual offers', *Journal of Psychology & Human Sexuality* 2 (1989): 39–55.

15 L. Al-Shawaf, D. M. Lewis and D. M. Buss, 'Sex differences in dis-gust: why are women more easily disgusted than men?', *Emotion Review* 10 (2018): 149–60.

16 Diane M. Kedzierski, *An Examination of Disgust, its Measures, and Gender Differences in the Experience of Disgust Sensitivity*. PhD dissertation, Nova Southeastern University, Florida, 2013; https://nsuworks.nova.edu/cps_stuetd/43.

17 Rachel Moran, *Paid For: My Journey through Prostitution*. Dublin: Gill & Macmillan, 2013.

18 See https://everydayfeminism.com/2016/07/feminist-hook-up -culture/; www.mic.com/articles/57795/your-7-point-intersect ional-feminist-guide-to-hook-ups.

19 Katie O'Malley and Becky Burgum, 'Demisexuality meaning and how it affects physical intimacy and attraction', 27 July 2021, www.elle.com/uk/life-and-culture/culture/a32765/what-it-mea ns-to-be-demisexual/.

20 See www.womenshealthmag.com/relationships/a30224236/casu al-sex-feelings/; www.vice.com/en/article/59mmzq/how-to-bio -hack-your-brain-to-have-sex-without-getting-emotionally-atta ched?utm_source=vicefbus; https://elle.in/article/how-to-have -casual-sex-without-getting-emotionally-attached-according-to -science/.

21 Justin R. Garcia et al., 'Sexual hookup culture: a review', *Review of General Psychology* 16 (2012): 161–76.

22 Lisa Wade, 'The rise of hookup culture on American college campuses', 25 August 2017, https://scholars.org/brief/rise-hoo kup-sexual-culture-american-college-campuses.

23 Leah Fessler, 'A lot of women don't enjoy hookup culture – so why do we force ourselves to participate?', 17 May 2016, https:// qz.com/685852/hookup-culture/.

24 R. L. Fielder and M. P. Carey, 'Prevalence and characteristics of sexual hookups among first-semester female college students', *Journal of Sex & Marital Therapy* 36 (2010): 346–59.

25 E. A. Armstrong, P. England and A. C. K. Fogarty, 'Accounting for women's orgasm and sexual enjoyment in college hookups and relationships', *American Sociological Review* 77 (2012): 435–62.

26 Caroline Heldman and Lisa Wade, 'Hook-up culture: setting a new research agenda', *Sexuality Research and Social Policy* 7 (2010): 323–33.

27 D. Herbenick, V. Schick, S. A. Sanders et al., 'Pain experienced

during vaginal and anal intercourse with other-sex partners: findings from a nationally representative probability study in the United States', *Journal of Sexual Medicine* 12 (2015): 1040–51.

28 R. Whitmire, 'A tough time to be a girl: gender imbalance on campuses', *Chronicle of Higher Education* 54 (2008): A23.

29 Heldman and Wade, 'Hook-up culture'.

30 David Buss and David Schmitt, 'Sexual strategies theory: an evolutionary perspective on human mating', *Psychological Review* 100 (1993): 204–32.

31 David Buss, *The Evolution of Desire: Strategies of Human Mating*. New York: Basic Books, [1994] 2016, p. 137.

32 Sherry Argov, *Why Men Love Bitches*. New York: Adams Media, p. 55.

33 Donald E. Brown, *Human Universals*. New York: McGraw-Hill, 1991.

34 Lawrence Stone, *The Road to Divorce: England 1530–1987*. Oxford: Oxford University Press, 1995, p. 7.

35 Anthony Giddens, *The Transformation of Intimacy: Sexuality, Love and Eroticism in Modern Societies*. Cambridge: Polity, 1992, p. 9.

36 Derek A. Kreager and Jeremy Staff, 'The sexual double standard and adolescent peer acceptance', *Social Psychology Quarterly* 72 (2009): 143–64.

37 Michael J. Marks, Tara M. Young and Yuliana Zaikman, 'The sexual double standard in the real world', *Social Psychology* 50 (2019): 67–79.

38 Daniel N. Jones, 'The "chasing Amy" bias in past sexual experiences: men can change, women cannot', *Sexuality & Culture* 20 (2016): 24–37.

39 Gillian Flynn, *Gone Girl*. New York: Crown, 2012.

40 See   www.reddit.com/r/relationships/comments/72115r/i25m _told_my_friends_with_benefits24f_i_dont_see/.

41 See   www.reddit.com/r/AmItheAsshole/comments/db03qr/ai ta_for_telling_my_fwb_that_i_think_she_should/.

42 Yanna J. Weisberg, Colin G. DeYoung and Jacob B. Hirsh,

'Gender differences in personality across the ten aspects of the Big Five', *Frontiers in Psychology* 2 (2011): 178; doi: 10.3389/fpsyg .2011.00178.

Chapter 5　Consent Is Not Enough

1　'An uncomfortable truth', www.youtube.com/watch?v-qrUiHB 5qJJ0.

2　*Generation Wealth*, director Lauren Greenfield, Evergreen Pictures, 2018.

3　Michelle Scalise Sugiyama, 'Fitness costs of warfare for women', *Human Nature* 25 (2014): 476–95.

4　'Linda Boreman, 53, star of "Deep Throat" became advocate against porn', 23 April 2002, www.latimes.com/archives/la-xpm-2002-apr-23-me-linda23-story.html.

5　Simon Garfield, 'Blow for freedom', 28 April 2002, www.theguar dian.com/film/2002/apr/28/features.review.

6　Linda Lovelace and Mike McGrady, *Ordeal: An Autobiography*. New York: Citadel Press, 1980.

7　See www.antipornography.org/racism-in-porn-industry-harsh -reality-exposed.html.

8　See www.antipornography.org/my-bulimia-eating-disorder-sto ry-how-it-harmed-me.html.

9　See www.antipornography.org/my story of becoming a metha mphetamine-addict.html.

10　See www.antipornography.org/female-porn-addiction-my-story -how-i-became-addict.html.

11　See www.antipornography.org/working-in-porn-is-a-dead-end -trip-to-nowhere.html.

12　See www.antipornography.org/is-doing-porn-empowering-for -women.html.

13　See www.stylist.co.uk/people/10-unlikely-oxford-union-spea kers/13301.

14　Ashley Maaike, 'Jenna Jameson is speaking out against trafficking in porn', 5 August 2020, https://filmdaily.co/news/jenna-james on-porn-trafficking/.

15 See https://filia.org.uk/resources/2020/5/16/international-call-for-credit-card-freeze-on-porn-sites.

16 David Auerbach, 'Vampire porn', 23 October 2014, https://web.archive.org/web/20141219160919/http://www.slate.com/artic les/technology/technology/2014/10/mindgeek_porn_monopo ly_its_dominance_is_a_cautionary_tale_for_other_industries .html.

17 Nicholas Kristof, 'The children of Pornhub', 4 December 2020, www.nytimes.com/2020/12/04/opinion/sunday/pornhub-rape -trafficking.html.

18 Nicholas Kristof, 'An uplifting update on the terrible world of Pornhub', 9 December 2020, www.nytimes.com/2020/12/09 /opinion/pornhub-news-child-abuse.html.

19 Kari Paul, 14 December 2020, www.theguardian.com/technolo gy/2020/dec/14/pornhub-purge-removes-unverified-videos-in vestigation-child-abuse.

20 Meg O'Connor, 18 October 2019, www.vice.com/en_uk/artic le/evjkdw/she-helped-expose-girls-do-porn-but-she-can-never -outrun-what-it-did-to-her.

21 Debbie L. Sklar, 12 April 2021, https://timesofsandiego.com/cr ime/2021/04/02/10-more-women-join-lawsuit-against-pornhub -plaintiffs-now-total-50/.

22 Ana Valens, 'Pornhub pulls Girls Do Porn videos amid sex traf-ficking charges', 15 October 2019, www.dailydot.com/irl/pornh ub-girls-do-porn-federal-charges/.

23 See www.10news.com/news/local-news/women-sue-pornhubs -parent-company-for-hosting-girlsdoporn-com-videos.

24 Sklar, 12 April 2021.

25 T. Jacobs, K. Fog-Poulsen, A. Vermandel et al., 'The effect of porn watching on erectile function', *European Urology Open Science* 19, Supplement e1121–e1122, July 2020.

26 See www.mirashowers.co.uk/blog/trends/revealed-what-brits-a re-really-getting-up-to-in-the-bathroom-1/.

27 Moya Lothian-McLean, 'How do your porn habits compare with

young people across Britain', 14 March 2019, www.bbc.co.uk/bb cthree/article/bb79a2ce-0de4-4965-98f0-9ebbcfcc2a60.

28 Interview with Fiona Vera Grey, 2 June 2020.

29 Charmaine Borg and Peter J. de Jong, 'Feelings of disgust and disgust-induced avoidance weaken following induced sexual arousal in women', *PLoS ONE* 7 (2012): e44111.

30 C. E. Ivan, 'On disgust and moral judgments: a review', *Journal of European Psychology Students* 6 (2015): 25–36.

31 David Courtwright, 31 May 2019, https://quillette.com/2019/05 /31/how-limbic-capitalism-preys-on-our-addicted-brains/.

32 Darryl T. Gwynne and David C. F. Rentz, 'Beetles on the bottle: male buprestids mistake stubbies for females (Coleoptera)', *Australian Journal of Entomology* 22 (1983): 79–80.

33 Diana Fleischman, 24 April 2018, https://jacobitemag.com/2018 /04/24/uncanny-vulvas/.

34 Amy Fleming, 'Is porn making young men impotent?', 11 March 2019, www.theguardian.com/lifeandstyle/2019/mar/11/young -men-porn-induced-erectile-dysfunction.

35 Brandon Griggs, 'Terry Crews: porn addiction "messed up my life"', 24 February 2016, https://edition.cnn.com/2016/02/24/en tertainment/terry-crews-porn-addiction-feat/index.html.

36 Venkatesh Rao, 17 August 2017, www.ribbonfarm.com/2017/08 /17/the-premium-mediocre-life-of-maya-millennial/.

37 Sarah Ditum, 26 June 2020, https://unherd.com/2020/06/why-doesnt-porn-ever-get-cancelled/.

38 Laura Mulvey, 'Visual pleasure and narrative cinema', *Screen* 16/3 (1975): 6–18.

Chapter 6 Violence Is Not Love

1 Gemma Askham, 'Ann Summers now has a real life Red Room', 11 April 2017, www.glamourmagazine.co.uk/article/fifty-shades -red-room-ann-summers.

2 Theodore Dalrymple, *Life at the Bottom: The Worldview that Makes the Underclass*. Chicago: Ivan R. Dee, 2001, pp. 75–6.

3 Ibid., p. 78.

4 Andreas Wismeijer and Marcel van Assen, 'Psychological characteristics of BDSM practitioners', *Journal of Sexual Medicine* 10 (2013): 1943–52.

5 Angela Carter, *The Sadeian Woman: An Exercise in Cultural History*. London: Virago, 1979 [Kindle edn, location 360].

6 Tony Perrottet, February 2015, www.smithsonianmag.com/history/who-was-marquis-de-sade-180953980/?all.

7 Ibid.

8 Gonzague Saint Bris, *Marquis de Sade: l'ange de l'ombre*. Paris: Editions Télémaque, 2013.

9 Perrottet, 2015.

10 Ibid.

11 Leland de la Durantaye, 'Who whips whom', *London Review of Books*, 19 February 2015.

12 Andrea Dworkin, *Pornography: Men Possessing Women*. New York: E. P. Dutton, [1979] 1989, p. 79.

13 Ibid., pp. 73–4.

14 Ibid., p. 89.

15 Roxane Gay, *Bad Feminist*. New York: HarperCollins, 2014, p. 184.

16 In Garth Greenwell and R. O. Kwon, eds, *Kink: Stories*. New York: Simon & Schuster, 2021.

17 Yvonne Roberts, 22 November 2020, www.theguardian.com/society/2020/nov/22/if-im-not-in-on-friday-i-might-be-dead-chilling-facts-about-uk-femicide.

18 Alys Harte, 'A man tried to choke me during sex without warning', 28 November 2019, www.bbc.com/news/uk-50546184.

19 Suzannah Weiss, 21 July 2020, https://www.menshealth.com/sex-women/a33382089/breath-play-erotic-asphyxiation-bdsm/.

20 See https://twitter.com/GigiEngle/status/1286391789352620044.

21 Helen Bichard, Christopher Byrne, Christopher W. N. Saville and Rudi Coetzer, 'The neuropsychological outcomes of non-fatal strangulation in domestic and sexual violence: a systematic review', *Neuropsychological Rehabilitation*, 12 January 2021.

22 Interview with Helen Bichard, 30 July 2020.

23 A. Coluccia, M. Gabbrielli, G. Gualtieri et al., 'Sexual masochism disorder with asphyxiophilia: a deadly yet underrecognized disease', *Case Reports in Psychiatry* (2016) article 5474862; www.hindawi.com/journals/crips/2016/5474862/.

24 Martine Berg Olsen, 26 June 2019, https://metro.co.uk/2019/06/26/webcam-girl-21-died-pervert-paid-strangle-watched-online-10077321/?ito=cbshare.

25 See www.endingtheviolence.us/articles.html.

26 Jonathan Herring, 'R v. Brown (1993)', in Philip Handler, Henry Mares and Ian Williams (eds), *Landmark Cases in Criminal Law*. Oxford: Hart, 2017, pp. 348–9.

27 Ibid., p. 350.

28 Kate Dennett, 23 July 2020, www.dailymail.co.uk/news/article-8552589/Businessman-killed-lover-used-rough-sex-defence-FREED-two-years.html.

29 Lucy Leeson and Danya Bazaraa, 20 August 2018, www.mirror.co.uk/news/uk-news/laura-huteson-death-killers-brutal-13109002.

30 See www.pressandjournal.co.uk/fp/news/aberdeen/1448323/sex-strangler-jailed-for-killing-20-year-old-chloe-miazek/.

31 Dennett, 23 July 2020.

32 Barbie Latza Nadeau, 5 February 2014, www.thedailybeast.com/iranian-found-in-venice-lagoon-alleged-victim-of-botched-sex-game?account=thedailybeast&medium=twitter&source=socialflow.

33 Will Stewart, 'Twisted torture', 27 August 2018, www.thesun.co.uk/news/7108595/suspect-paedo-dumps-teens-body-pavement-bdsm/.

34 Richard Hartley-Parkinson, 18 May 2016, https://metro.co.uk/2016/05/18/psychologist-dies-after-asking-flatmate-to-strangle-her-during-sex-5889007/.

35 See www.pnn.de/kultur/ueberregional/trauerspiel-alexander-und-natalia-ein/21848546.html [in German].

36 Serina Sandhu, 24 September 2015, www.independent.co.uk/ne

ws/world/americas/us-man-disembowels-woman-uttering-wro
ng-name-during-sex-10512965.html.

37 Fiona MacKenzie, 'We Can't Consent To This' briefing docu-
ment, 2020; see https://wecantconsenttothis.uk/press.

38 Rosamund Urwin and Esmé O'Keeffe, 26 January 2020, www.the
times.co.uk/article/social-media-make-girls-think-choking-duri
ng-sex-is-normal-0jlrgf2b0.

39 Interview with Clare McGlynn, 29 May 2020.

40 Dolly Alderton, 18 April 2021, www.thetimes.co.uk/article/dear
-dolly-im-a-feminist-so-why-am-i-only-attracted-to-misogynis
ts-20cgws8z8.

41 'Grime artist Solo 45 "choked woman with collar"', 16 December
2019, www.bbc.co.uk/news/uk-england-bristol-50816008; 'Grime
artist Solo 45 "waterboarded victim"', 28 November 2019,
www.bbc.co.uk/news/uk-england-bristol-50591539; 'Grime artist Solo 45 "held gun to head of rape victim"', 6 December 2019,
www.bbc.co.uk/news/uk-england-bristol-50690488; 'Solo 45 trial:
grime artist a "narcissist and bully"', 12 February 2020, www.
bbc.co.uk/news/uk-england-bristol-51478517; Geoffrey Bennett,
30 July 2020, www.bristolpost.co.uk/news/bristol-news/solo-45-
rape-court-case-4378719.

42 Claire Hayhurst and Emma Flanagan, 24 February 2020, www
.bristolpost.co.uk/news/bristol-news/solo-45s-defence-claims
-four-3881370; 'Solo 45 trial: grime artist jailed for raping four
women', 30 July 2020, www.bbc.co.uk/news/uk-england-bristol
-53593983.

43 See   www.enfieldindependent.co.uk/news/18229785.police-pus
hed-woman-allege-raped-grime-artist-solo-45-court-told/.

Chapter 7 People Are Not Products

1 Helen Mathers, *Josephine Butler: Patron Saint of Prostitutes*.
Stroud: History Press, 2014, p. 165.

2 Ibid.

3 Ibid., p. 129.

4 Ibid., p. 165.

5 Alison Phipps, *Me, Not You: The Trouble with Mainstream Feminism*. Manchester: Manchester University Press, 2020 [Kindle edn, location 1873].

6 Antoinette M. Burton, 'The white woman's burden: British feminists and the Indian woman, 1865–1915', *Women's Studies International Forum* 13 (1990): 295–308.

7 Kate Lister, 'Sex and money', in *A Curious History of Sex*. London: Unbound, 2020.

8 Meena Seshu and Aarthi Pai, 'Sex work undresses patriarchy with every trick!', *IDS Bulletin* 45 (2014): 46–52.

9 David Buss, *Bad Men: The Hidden Roots of Sexual Deception, Harassment and Assault*. London: Robinson, 2021, pp. 15–16.

10 Rachel Moran, *Paid For: My Journey through Prostitution*. Cork: Gill & Macmillan, 2013, pp. 112–13.

11 Sam Greenhill, 26 June 2010, www.dailymail.co.uk/sciencetech /article-1289603/Romans-killed-100-unwanted-babies-English -brothel.html.

12 F. H. Ampt, L. Willenberg, P. A. Agius et al., 'Incidence of unintended pregnancy among female sex workers in low-income and middle-income countries: a systematic review and meta-analysis', *BMJ Open* 8 (2018): e021779; doi: 10.1136/bmjopen-2018-021779.

13 Juno Mac and Molly Smith, *Revolting Prostitutes: The Fight for Sex Workers' Rights*. London: Verso, 2018, p. 18.

14 Julie Bindel, *The Pimping of Prostitution: Abolishing the Sex Work Myth*. Basingstoke: Palgrave Macmillan, 2017, p. 60.

15 Douglas Fox, 'Don't criminalise our clients', 19 November 2008, www.theguardian.com/profile/douglas-fox.

16 Bindel, *The Pimping of Prostitution*, p. 22.

17 Elizabeth Bernstein, 'What's wrong with prostitution? What's right with sex work? Comparing markets in female sexual labor', *Hastings Women's Law Journal* 10 (1999): 91–.

18 Emily Bazelon, 'Should prostitution be a crime?', *New York Times*, 5 May 2016.

19 See https://quillette.com/2019/11/16/thorstein-veblens-theory -of-the-leisure-class-a-status-update/.

20 'Prostitution – the facts', 2015, www.streetlight.uk.com/the-fa
cts/.

21 Meredith H. Lair, *Armed with Abundance: Consumerism and Soldiering in the Vietnam War*. Chapel Hill: University of North Carolina Press, 2011, p. 207.

22 Ibid.

23 Jean Enriquez, 'Globalization, militarism and sex trafficking', 10 November 2006, https://sisyphe.org/spip.php?article2475.

24 Bindel, *The Pimping of Prostitution*, p. 132.

25 S. Cunningham, T. Sanders, L. Platt et al., 'Sex work and occupational homicide: analysis of a U.K. murder database', *Homicide Studies* 22 (2018): 321–38.

26 John J. Potterat, Devon D. Brewer, Stephen Q. Muth et al., 'Mortality in a long-term open cohort of prostitute women', *American Journal of Epidemiology* 159 (2004): 778–85.

27 Brooke Magnanti, *The Sex Myth: Why Everything We're Told Is Wrong*. London: Weidenfeld & Nicolson, 2012.

28 Tiggey May, Alex Harocopos and Michael Hough, *For Love or Money: Pimps and the Management of Sex Work*. London: Home Office, 2000.

29 S. Adriaenssens and J. Hendrickx, 'What can internet data tell about safe work? Unsafe sex and contract breach as proxies of quality of work in prostitution', COST ProsPol Action meeting, Ljubljana, 2016.

30 Ibid.

31 Aaron Sibarium, 23 September 2020, https://americancompass .org/the-commons/three-theses-about-cuties/.

32 Ali Pantony, 24 April 2017, www.glamourmagazine.co.uk/article /sex-for-rent.

33 Harvey Jones, 2 April 2018, www.theguardian.com/money/20 18/apr/02/sex-for-rent-accommodation-rogue-landlords-cam paign.

34 Nigel Lewis, 10 June 2021, www.landlordzone.co.uk/news/labo ur-seeks-mps-support-for-specific-offence-of-sex-for-rent/.

35   See   https://twitter.com/libdems/status/1221842805607276545
     ?lang=en.

36   Ibid.

37   'Support for survivors who are or have been involved in the sex
     industry', 2021, www.rasasc.org.uk/e-newsletter/outreach-with
     -women-in-sex-work/.

38   See www.libdems.org.uk/f9_towards_safer_sex_work.

39   Rowena Mason, 4 March 2016, www.theguardian.com/politics
     /2016/mar/04/jeremy-corbyn-decriminalise-sex-industry-prosti
     tution.

40   Susie Coen and Talya Varga, 1 January 2021, www.dailymail.co
     .uk/news/article-9105215/Preyed-sex-rent-landlords-Men-tou
     ting-rooms-exchange-sexual-favours.html.

41   Robin Hanson, 26 April 2018, www.overcomingbias.com/2018
     /04/two-types-of-envy.html.

42   Jordan Weissmann, 28 April 2018, https://slate.com/business
     /2018/04/economist-robin-hanson-might-be-americas-creepi
     est-professor.html.

43   Moira Donegan, 'Actually we don't owe you sex, and we never
     will', 4 May 2018, www.cosmopolitan.com/politics/a20138446
     /redistribution-sex-incels/.

44   Vednita Carter, 'The pimping of prostitution', www.youtube.com
     /watch?v=2Y-VmuKmsP0.

45   Arwa Mahdawi, 'The WAP uproar shows conservatives are fine
     with female sexuality – as long as men control it', 15 August
     2020, www.theguardian.com/commentisfree/2020/aug/15/cardi
     -b-megan-thee-stallion-wap-conservatives-female-sexuality.

46   Mathers, *Josephine Butler*, p. 165.

47   See https://invisible-men-canada.tumblr.com.

48   Thomas Hollands, 24 April 2020, https://xsrus.com/the-econo
     mics-of-onlyfans.

49   Emily Ratajkowski, *My Body*. London: Quercus, 2021, p. 102.

50   Quoted in James Mumford, *Vexed: Ethics Beyond Political Tribes*.
     London: Bloomsbury Continuum, 2020, pp. 77–8.

51 See www.humanetech.com/app-ratings.

52 Andre Shakti, '8 very necessary sex tips from sex workers', 30 October 2015, www.cosmopolitan.com/sex-love/news/a48407 /sex-tips-from-sex-workers/; '5 insightful sex tips from a professional sex worker', https://thoughtcatalog.com/melanie-ber liet/2014/10/5-insightful-sex-tips-from-a-professional-sex-wor ker/.

Chapter 8 Marriage Is Good

1 Aidan Lyon, 'Why are normal distributions normal?', *British Journal for the Philosophy of Science* 65 (2014): 621–49.

2 H. J. Eysenck and James A. Wakefield, 'Psychological factors as predictors of marital satisfaction', *Advances in Behaviour Research and Therapy* 3 (1981): 151–92.

3 Jane Galt [Megan McArdle], 'A really, really, really long post about gay marriage that does not, in the end, support one side or the other', 2 April 2005, https://web.archive.org/web/200504 06215537/http://www.janegalt.net/blog/archives/005244.html.

4 Hansard, House of Lords debates, vol. 303, col. 297, 30 June 1969.

5 Gavin Thompson et al., *Olympic Britain: Social and Economic Change since the 1908 and 1948 London Games*. London: House of Commons Library, 2011.

6 Chiara Giordano, 'UK heterosexual marriage rate falls to lowest on record', 14 April 2020, www.independent.co.uk/news/uk/ho me-news/marriage-rate-uk-latest-figures-lowest-record-ons-a9 464706.html.

7 Births in England and Wales: summary tables, Office for National Statistics, Release date: 22 July 2020.

8 Thompson et al., *Olympic Britain*.

9 Dan Hurley, 19 April 2005, www.nytimes.com/2005/04/19/heal th/divorce-rate-its-not-as-high-as-you-think.html.

10 W. Bradford Wilcox and Wendy Wang, 25 September 2017, https://ifstudies.org/blog/the-marriage-divide-how-and-why-working-class-families-are-more-fragile-today.

11 Susan B. Sorenson and Devan Spear, 'New data on intimate partner violence and intimate relationships: implications for gun laws and federal data collection', *Preventive Medicine* 107 (2018): 103–8.

12 Paul Amato and Alan Booth, *A Generation at Risk: Growing Up in an Era of Family Upheaval*. Cambridge, MA: Harvard University Press, 1997, p. 220.

13 Paula Span, 'The gray gender gap: older women are likelier to go it alone', 11 October 2016, www.nytimes.com/2016/10/11/heal th/marital-status-elderly-health.html; Kyrsty Hazell, 31 January 2012, www.huffingtonpost.co.uk/2012/01/31/divorced-men-are -twice-as-likely-to-remarry_n_1243472.html.

14 Sonia Frontera, 4 August 2021, www.divorcemag.com/blog/if-you-divorce-now-will-you-regret-your-divorce-later.

15 Betsey Stevenson, 'The impact of divorce laws on marriage-specific capital', *Journal of Labor Economics* 25 (2007): 75–94.

16 Nicola Davis and Niamh McIntyre, 7 March 2019, www.theguar dian.com/uk-news/2019/mar/07/revealed-pill-still-most-popul ar-prescribed-contraceptive-in-england; Kimberly Daniels and Joyce C. Abma, 'Current contraception status among women aged 15–49', December 2018, www.cdc.gov/nchs/products/da tabriefs/db327.htm.

17 'How effective is contraception at preventing pregnancy?', 17 April 2020, www.nhs.uk/conditions/contraception/how-effective-contraception/.

18 See www.guttmacher.org/news-release/2018/about-half-us-abo rtion-patients-report-using-contraception-month-they-became.

19 Virginia Ironside, 18 January 2011, www.dailymail.co.uk/home /you/article-1346813/The-flip-1960s-sexual-revolution-We-pa id-price-free-love.html.

20 Nikola Komlenac, Manuel Pittl, Susanne Perkhofer et al., 'Links between virginity beliefs, negative feelings after virginity loss and sexual performance anxiety in a sample of German-speaking heterosexual-identified women and men', *Journal of Sex & Marital Therapy* 48 (2022): 1–18.

21 See www.youtube.com/watch?v=MoudH-RPnEE.

22 Hansard, House of Commons debates, vol. 561, col. 229, 15 April 2013.

23 Timothy Grall, 'Custodial mothers and fathers and their child support: 2015', January 2020, www.census.gov/content/dam /Census/library/publications/2020/demo/p60-262.pdf.

24 Sara McLanahan and Gary D. Sandefur, *Growing Up with a Single Parent: What Hurts, What Helps*. Cambridge, MA: Harvard University Press, 1994, p. 1.

25 Cynthia C. Harper and Sara S. McLanahan, 'Father absence and youth incarceration', *Journal of Research on Adolescence* 14 (2004): 369–97.

26 McLanahan and Sandefur, *Growing Up with a Single Parent*.

27 Nicholas Zill and Charlotte A. Schoenborn, *Developmental, Learning, and Emotional Problems: Health of Our Nation's Children, United States, 1988*. Hyattsville, MD: National Center for Health Statistics, 1990, p. 9.

28 Steven Pinker, *How the Mind Works*. New York: W. W. Norton, 2009, p. 434.

29 Martin Daly and Margo Wilson, 'The "Cinderella effect" is no fairy tale', *Trends in Cognitive Sciences* 9 (2005): 507–8.

30 Lara Bazelon, 'Divorce can be an act of radical self-love', 30 September 2021, www.nytimes.com/2021/09/30/opinion/divor ce-children.html.

31 Quoted in Diane Jeske and Richard Fumerton, eds, *Readings in Political Philosophy: Theory and Applications*. Peterborough, Ont.: Broadview Press, 2011, p. 649.

32 *The Hostel for Homeless Young Mums*, episode 1, BBC Three, 7 June 2019.

33 Barbara A. Crow, *Radical Feminism: A Documentary Reader*. New York: New York University Press, 2000, p. 76.

34 Amy Westervelt, 26 May 2018, www.theguardian.com/com mentisfree/2018/may/26/is-motherhood-the-unfinished-work -of-feminism.

35 Mary Ann Mason, 'In the ivory tower, men only', 17 June 2013,

https://slate.com/human-interest/2013/06/female-academics
-pay-a-heavy-baby-penalty.html.

36 Leah Libresco Sargeant, 7 December 2020, www.plough.com/en
/topics/justice/culture-of-life/dependence.

37 Susan Faludi, 8 April 2013, www.newyorker.com/magazine/2013
/04/15/death-of-a-revolutionary.

38 *As You Like It*, Act II, scene VII.

39 Germaine Greer, *The Female Eunuch*. London: Harper Perennial,
[1970] 2006, pp. 264–6.

40 Nicholas A. Christakis, *Blueprint: The Evolutionary Origins of a
Good Society*. New York: Little, Brown, 2019, p. 74.

41 Patrick Lee, Robert P. George and Gerard V. Bradley, 'Marriage
and procreation', 28 March 2011, www.thepublicdiscourse.com
/2011/03/2638/.

42 Eli J. Finkel, *The All-or-Nothing Marriage: How the Best Marriages
Work*. New York: Dutton, 2017.

43 John Corvino and Maggie Gallagher, *Debating Same-Sex
Marriage*. New York: Oxford University Press, 2012.

44 Mary Harrington, 21 October 2020, https://unherd.com/2020
/10/feminists-shouldnt-have-sex-before-marriage/.

45 Erika Bachiochi, *The Rights of Women: Reclaiming a Lost
Vision*. Notre Dame, IN: University of Notre Dame Press, 2021,
p. 16.

46 D. R. White, L. Betzig, M. B. Mulder et al., 'Rethinking polygyny:
co-wives, codes, and cultural systems' (and comments and reply),
Current Anthropology 29 (1988): 529–72; www.jstor.org/stable
/2743506.

47 Joseph Henrich, Robert Boyd and Peter J. Richerson, 'The puzzle
of monogamous marriage', *Philosophical Transactions of the
Royal Society B: Biological Sciences* 367 (2012): 657–69.

48 Lee Gettler, Thomas McDade, Alan Feranil and Christopher
Kuzawa, 'Longitudinal evidence that fatherhood decreases testosterone in human males', *Proceedings of the National Academy
of Sciences of the United States of America* 108 (2011): 16194–9.

49 Jennifer Savin, 'Would you sign a sexual consent form?',

13 March 2020, www.cosmopolitan.com/uk/love-sex/sex/a310
42298/sexual-consent-forms/.

50 See https://twitter.com/juliaioffe/status/1446113958650253313.

Conclusion

1 See https://defaultfriend.substack.com/p/72-the-coming-wave
-of-sex-negativity/comments.

2 www.tiktok.com/@boopyshmurda/video/70056691467971002
94?_d=secCgwIARCbDRjEFSACKAESPgo8A3%2F3%2BVqr99y
p38CjHMwIHZRovbGpN%2F1Ofceit60%2FbrIkip5j1wjtLbaWk
NvIMMYfq7cfVOfZYKXnj8OFGgA%3D&checksum=efde3365
a11e4446425e803bb2365a4bc7da8adc77b611ca58eea8c386503
010&language=en&preview_pb=0&sec_user_id=MS4wLjABAA
AAF6zaqMYfQnKJ0VNVgzQZ_iQZLpCAwXeTp-B4vxjUUhm
Gv-0l5ymJtF7GB2x7PqDr&share_app_id=1233&share_item_id
=7005669146797100294&share_link_id=F9BB5F9F-0B51-4FC9
-8E3A-465856C0AF34&source=h5_m&timestamp=163926026
4&tt_from=copy&u_code=djbm55jfm1c18g&user_id=6980252
324338697221&utm_campaign=client_share&utm_medium=io
s&utm_source=copy&_r=1.